There's nothing like the rich aroma of freshly brewed coffee in the morning—but there's so much more to coffee than that first cup of the day!

The Coffee Book is a complete guide to buying, brewing, and enjoying the unique and incomparable flavor of coffee—and also includes exciting recipes for such coffee-inspired treats as . . .

- Bananas Foster Espresso
- Coffee-Spiked Pasta Sauce
- Thai Peanut Sauce with Coffee
- Coffee Crème Anglaise
- Espresso-Anise Wafers
- Butterscotch Coffee Squares
- Cappuccino Pound Cake
- Coffee Egg Cream

and many more

THE COFFEE BOOK

THE COFFEE BOOK

MELISSA CLARK

Produced by The Philip Lief Group, Inc.

BERKLEY BOOKS, NEW YORK

FOR MY MOTHER,
WITH WHOM I DRINK TEA

THE COFFEE BOOK

A Berkley Book / published by arrangement with
The Philip Lief Group, Inc.

PRINTING HISTORY
Berkley edition / January 1994

BERKLEY®
Berkley Books are published by
The Berkley Publishing Group, 200 Madison Avenue,
New York, New York 10016.
BERKLEY and the "B" design are trademarks of
Berkley Publishing Corporation.

PRINTED IN THE UNITED STATES OF AMERICA

10 9 8 7 6 5 4 3 2 1

CONTENTS

LIST OF COFFEE-INSPIRED RECIPES

BEVERAGES

PUDDINGS AND SOUFFLÉS

Crème Brûlée au Café
Caramelized Espresso-Chestnut Soufflé
Coffee-Hazelnut Soufflés with Cognac Sauce
Mocha Cinnamon Mousse with Toasted Almonds
Coffee-Cardamom Parfait

FRUIT DESSERTS

Fall Fruit Compote with Red Wine and Coffee
Coffee-Poached Seckel Pears
Fresh Cherries with Espresso and Brandy
Orange Salad with Walnuts, Dates, and
   Spiced Coffee Syrup
Gingered Cranberry Relish with Coffee
Bananas Foster Espresso
Blueberry Plum Preserves

CANDIES

Coffee Toffee Pecan
Espresso Truffles
Tender Coffee Caramels
Mocha Pistachio Fudge
Coffee–Pine Nut Pralines

DESSERT SAUCES

Coffee Crème Anglaise
Coffee-Flavored Honey Sauce
Coffee Syrup
Coffee-Flavored Sabayon Sauce
Mocha Sauce

MAIN COURSES

Lamb Stew with Vegetables and Coffee
Risotto with Cabbage and Sausage
Curried Chicken Breasts with Figs
Steak au Poivre et Café
Swordfish Steaks with Ginger, Orange, and Coffee

VEGETABLES AND SIDE DISHES

Coffee Guacamole
Orange Coffee Beets
Carrot Raisin Salad with Cardamom and Coffee
Nutted Wild Rice with Espresso
Cold Broccoli Salad with Cumin

SAUCES

Coffee-Spiked Pasta Sauce
Coffee-Chive Sauce
Roasted Walnut Pesto
Red Wine Sauce with Coffee
"Wild" Mushroom Sauce
Thai Peanut Sauce with Coffee
Coffee-Peanut Mayonnaise
Coffee Oil
Coffee Vinaigrette
Coffee-Flavored Vinegar

INTRODUCTION

Although I have presumed to write a book on coffee, I must confess that for most of my life I was an affirmed tea drinker. This is not to say that I never liked coffee; I loved it in Europe—dark, rich espresso served in tiny cups; milky café au lait in deep round bowls, and frothy cappuccino with its cocoa-laden foam. However, the coffee I was used to ordering as a pick-me-up in New York diners was bland and bitter by comparison.

It wasn't until I spent some time in the Pacific Northwest that I started to adore coffee in America. It was better than anything I had ever had, even in Europe. I wanted it all the time, every which way. Plain, with cold milk, steamed milk, or chocolate; even the decaffeinated varieties tasted good. But I never drank coffee in New York because I didn't know where to find the best coffee.

It really took a while before I thought to buy the beans from one of my favorite coffeehouses in Seattle and brew the drink myself at home. Coffee was never something I made at home, unless guests preferred it to tea. I didn't think I could do it without the proper equipment: the espresso machine with an attached milk steamer; the fancy French press pot; the Swiss gold filter cone. I did have a coffee grinder, an ancient housewarming gift from my parents, but it just sat in the back of the cupboard until I needed it to grind spices for an elaborate Indian dinner or nuts for a torte. I had never ground coffee in it, since I always bought my coffee a pound at a time, had it ground at the store, and froze it until coffee-drinking company appeared. Sometimes the bag lasted for six months to a year, and I had one bag of decaffeinated Viennese roast in my freezer for about two and half years, which I probably would have served had someone asked for it. My guests never complained, but, come to think of it, they never asked for seconds, either.

My discovery that I could make good coffee at home came, like most great things, accidentally. While in Seattle one summer I received a request from a more coffee-literate friend for a pound of Starbuck's House Blend in the bean. I decided to buy a pound for myself as well, having enjoyed two or three cups of the brew each day during my visit. I bought it on the way to the airport, two bags fresh-roasted, and made my first cup about eighteen hours later after grinding the beans in my neglected mill, measuring carefully, and remembering something I'd heard about the proper water temperature being just under boiling. I took as much care with my coffee as I did with my tea, and—unbelievably—the result tasted good. Very good with hot milk and sugar, but best just plain. I was on to something big.

Once the pound was gone, my next task was to find something equally good in New York. This was not easy several years ago, though it is getting easier now. Almost every corner deli sells ''gourmet'' coffees, which are displayed in plastic bins behind the counter, but these are often inferior beans that have grown stale with age. Nothing to compare to beans roasted within days or even hours before purchase. Luckily I found some dedicated roasters right here in New York, including Oren's Daily Roast, Porto

Rico, and Gillies, who are all committed to selling excellent beans. But even if you have no local coffee source, several of the better roasters—including those I just mentioned, and others like Starbuck's of Seattle and Coffee Connection of Brighton, Massachusetts—now have mail-order services, with vacuum packaging that ensures freshness.

Tea is still my preferred morning brew, but coffee at noon keeps me well charged for the rest of the day, with decaf filling in after dark. I don't know how I ever lived happily without it.

PART ONE

PART ONE

* * *

ALL ABOUT COFFEE

THE HISTORY OF COFFEE

To explore the exotic and little known history of coffee, a history reaching back almost one thousand years and traversing continents and cultures, one must be ready to indulge in colorful fantasy. How did the pit of a sweet fruit end up as the source of one of the most widely consumed beverages in the world? The path is twisted and often unbelievable, fact and fiction forever intermingled and united.

The stories told about the earliest uses of coffee are no more than entertaining conjecture, since there are no writings and little archaeological evidence on the subject. One idyll that I particularly like runs along the same lines as the tales of Marie Antoinette's flirtation with the pastoral life of the wandering shepherdess. It is said that a nomadic shepherd named Kaldi took his flock foraging far from their familiar fields during a drought. He noticed that after his goats had eaten the berries and leaves of a certain tree, they were friskier and more frolicsome than usual. So the shepherd himself sampled a few berries, and soon he too felt like dancing across the fields.

News of the magical berry went far, and according to another source, it soon became customary to crush the berries and roll them in animal fat to make small nuggets, which the nomads carried with them as high-energy snacks. This is probably a very early relative of our gorp. It has been suggested that the early coffee-berry eaters might also have made wine out of the fermented berries, but this is most likely a misinterpretation of the Arabic word for coffee, *qahwa,* which at one time, before coffee made its appearance in the Arab world, also meant "wine."

The earliest references to coffee (*qahwa*) in Arab literature date back to the latter half of the fifteenth century. The first coffee quaffers of the Arab world were members of the Sufi Muslim sect from Yemen, who used coffee not as beverage but as a drug that would keep them awake and alert during their long evening prayers. The bean was brought to them, as one version goes, by a scholar named Dhabhani. Dhabhani was sent to Ethiopia where he witnessed the use of the coffee berry for medicinal purposes. When Dhabhani returned to Yemen, he fell ill, and took coffee in an attempt to cure himself. Coffee not only cured him of his illness but also gave him additional energy for his devotions. The use of coffee soon became widespread among the Sufi.

Several things are unclear in this tale. For example, did Dhabhani bring home to Yemen the coffee beans from Ethiopia and then decide to try them, or were they already growing in Yemen, but had never before been consumed by humans (or formerly lethargic goats)? The sources say that the people of Ethiopia took coffee as a medicine, but how? As a food? Or did they make a beverage of it? And how did the Sufis take coffee? When were the beans first roasted, pounded, and boiled to produce the heavenly drink we recognize today? None of these questions have exact answers, but we do know that coffee was prepared as we know it by the late sixteenth century, as we have several accounts from European travelers describing Arabs imbibing a "sooty syrup" made from "burnt" seeds. Needless to say, it was several more years before Europeans embraced the drink themselves.

Further problems in pinning down the origins of coffee stem from the misinterpretation surrounding the word *qahwa*, mentioned above. Since the word, at one time, meant "wine" and was used frequently in Arabic texts, some scholars have mistakenly assumed that coffee has been around a lot longer than it in fact has. Another misunderstanding came from the Arabic word *quwwa*, meaning "power and strength." This word is often cited as the root of our words, "coffee," and it is easily associated with coffee's invigorating effects. Finally, there is Kaffa, a region in Ethiopia where coffee might have been discovered. Reading any Arabic text and confusing all these similar words has led many a scholar down a dead end.

Timothy Castle, in his book *The Perfect Cup,* brings up another important theory about the origins of coffee. He suggests that it was perhaps the women of Ethiopia who first made use of the coffee plant. This rings true when one considers that historically women have been the primary gatherers in a hunter-gatherer society. They were also generally responsible for the preparation of food and drink. However, the first students of the history of coffee were interested not in the origin of the drink but rather in how coffee developed as a favorite beverage in their particular society. Thus, one has the Arabs writing about Sufi scholars bringing the bean from the "nonentities" in Ethiopia, and then the Europeans adopting the drink of "those Arabs." Neither society has given much care to what happened before they "civilized" the drink in their own culture.

So romantic legends and conjecture must serve instead of fact to get to the deep root of the coffee plant.

When coffee did finally make its European debut, it was

introduced as a medicine—a regular panacea. It was given credit for curing a great variety of illnesses. The people of Europe were only later to learn that the people of the Arab nations drank coffee because they liked its flavor rather than as a medicine. By the time the Europeans developed a taste for the brew, the Arabs had already established a monopoly on the coffee-bean trade. They went so far to guard "their" bean that they banned the export of all "live" coffee beans—that is, beans that could germinate and grow into coffee trees. To prevent this, beans were boiled or roasted before being shipped to Europe. All visitors were forbidden to visit coffee plantations lest they abscond with a pocketful of sacred seeds or cuttings.

Inevitably, with so many pilgrims trampling the fields on their way to Mecca, some of the beans escaped. The first live coffee plant brought to Europe in 1616 was purportedly smuggled in by the Dutch who obtained it from pilgrims in India. Over the next seventy years, the Dutch cultivated thriving plantations all over Indonesia, and coffee became firmly ensconced as the favorite beverage of the Netherlands.

Not surprisingly, the French tell an intensely romantic story about their first coffee plant. It was presented as a gift from the mayor of Amsterdam to Louis XIV in 1714. The Sun King carefully cultivated this seedling in his Jardin des Plantes in Paris. However, it was the patriotic fervor of a young sailor from Normandy, Gabriel Mathieu de Clieu, who determined that France should begin coffee production in its Caribbean colonies. How did he obtain the clipping that would flourish and multiply into hundreds of plantations all over the West Indies and South America from the well-guarded royal coffee trees? That's where the romanticizing begins. Some sources allude to an elicit relationship between de Clieu and a lady of high rank. Others recount gallant missions in the night. Bribery is a logical option as well. But no one knows for certain.

Then there is the intriguing story of Brazil's coffee acquisition, made through a handsome Spanish colonel, Francisco de Melo Palheta. This gentleman is rumored to have received a cutting of the plant from the wife of the governor of French Guiana, who supposedly secreted it in a bouquet of flowers she sent to the gallant swain. This seedling, an offspring of the original one from Louis XIV's garden, then went on to populate Brazil and Colombia, two of today's largest coffee-producing nations of the world.

So next time you swallow a mouthful of hot coffee, reflect on its long and diverse history. Isn't it still slightly romantic to think of your beans as having an ancestry comparable to royalty?

THE RISE AND FALL OF THE COFFEEHOUSE CULTURE

Coffee has always been a social drink, even from the very beginning of its acceptance into the religious ceremony of the Sufi Muslims. In Muslim society, coffee was the most logical substitute for wine, which is forbidden by the Koran. Worshipers took to the drink because it helped them stay awake for their nighttime prayers and studies. They formally gathered together to drink coffee before prayer, and coffee assumed the status of a communal beverage. European travelers noted that Arab men shared one or two coffee cups, which they passed around a circle after taking a small sip. Nobody kept a cup to himself or refused his neighbor a draft.

When coffee made its debut in secular spheres, it was only natural that it would keep its communal overtones and ceremony. Hence the rise of the coffeehouse in Arab culture—a place where men could gather to drink coffee and soberly discuss a wide range of intellectual topics. Westerner visitors noted the code of etiquette surrounding the making and presentation of coffee, including much bowing, toasting, and honoring one's companions. It took several decades of avid coffee consumption for the drink to reach the domestic circle, but when it did, it remained a social beverage. Coffee was not drunk alone; it was offered to honored guests as a sign of hospitality. It was considered an outrage not to drink coffee with one's host and an even greater social sin for a host not to offer it.

In a café, strangers vied for the opportunity to buy each another a cup of coffee, and even today in smaller villages in Turkey, it is not unheard of to sit down in a café and have one's coffee paid for by a complete stranger.

When coffee found its way to Europe, it came not merely as a beverage but as a social diversion as well. In London and Paris, coffeehouses opened en masse in the seventeenth century. Café Procope, which was established in Paris in 1689 is still serving tiny cups of coffee today; mirrors, marble, and velvet evoke the mystery and luxury of its past. It is said that in London around the year 1700 there were close to three thousand coffeehouses—an enormous number, considering that the population of the city was then only 600,000. And since women were barred from patronizing them, this number was actually closer to 300,000. This assumes about one coffeehouse for every 100 people. Even if this figure is exaggerated, it still shows the enormity of the trend.

As Wolfgang Schivelbusch theorizes in his book *Tastes of Paradise*, coffee served many functions in European society. It replaced beer and wine as the beverage of choice in all social classes, starting in the court and trickling down to the bourgeoisie and eventually to the poorer classes. Before the introduction of coffee, tea, and chocolate, people had no great access to nonalcoholic beverages, especially city folk who lacked access to clean water and fresh milk. Hard cider, beer, and wine were the staple beverages. Beer, with its high carbohydrate content also functioned as a major source of nourishment in northern countries such as England, Holland, Belgium, and Germany.

The acceptance of coffee into the mainstream coincided with the growth of Protestantism and its work ethic.

Whereas workers formerly had begun their day with a hearty bowl of beer soup, they now drank coffee, which was sobering and stimulating. Regular ingestion meant more reliable workers and greater profits. This economic factor is probably one of the most important reasons that coffee was so universally accepted. Taverns closed and reopened as coffeehouses where businessmen could socialize, work, and stay sober at the same time.

Coffeehouses, especially in England, were so connected to the idea of work that one, Lloyd's Coffeehouse, eventually evolved into Lloyd's of London, one of the world's largest insurance firms. Lloyd's is a representative story. As a coffeehouse located close to London's ports, it became known as a gathering place for ship owners, captains, merchants, and insurance brokers who would underwrite voyages. Some businessmen even rented out specific booths in coffeehouses, where they would conduct their daily affairs. Before the institution of reliable daily papers, coffeehouses were also the center for news, and Lloyd's even published its own journal at one time.

Because coffeehouses functioned partly as the newsrooms, they tended to attract intellectuals and political writers who needed to be kept informed. As this more cerebral community grew, coffeehouses became a haven where writers could discuss their work and ideas as they sipped their brew. Rumor has it that Voltaire wrote and discussed much of his work in coffeehouses, where he drank an average of forty cups a day!

Since men were spending so much of their time in coffeehouses, it was not surprising that the women who were barred from these social hubs would rebel. In 1674 a group of London women published a ''Women's Petition Against Coffee,'' which blamed the drink for their husbands' lack of virility. King Charles II also tried in vain to ban the bean, saying it distracted citizens from their civil and familial duties.

The real reason for the decrease in the popularity of England's coffeehouses had less to do with these complaints than with economics. Coffee was never taken up as a plantation crop in any of Britain's colonies, as it was in the colonies of France and Holland. The East India Tea Company, however, saw the benefits of importing tea from India to England. And tea—without all of the historic social baggage surrounding coffee—was a drink that could be enjoyed by both sexes together.

Eventually, coffeehouses were turned into men's clubs where business was conducted. Tea was taken at home with the family. It was a compromise: men divided their time between family and society instead of isolating themselves in coffeehouses.

In France, Holland, and Germany, coffee had always been enjoyed by both sexes. In Holland and Germany, it was commonly prepared at home by the women and came to symbolize the comforts of domestic life. The contented family seated around a coffee table was a common subject for family portraits. In France, coffeehouses were respectable social gathering places patronized by men and women of several classes. As long as one could pay for a cup, one was not turned away.

Despite its popularity in Germany, coffee was banned there by Frederick the Great. Since Germany, unlike Holland and France, did not have any coffee-producing colonies and never developed a taste for tea, it had to buy coffee through a series of middlemen at greatly inflated prices. Frederick the Great was reported to have gone so far in his prohibitive tactics as to send out official coffee sniffers to patrol the city streets, sniffing for the distinctive aroma of roasting coffee. Offenders were fined and, in a few cases, even imprisoned.

Germans began drinking chicory coffee as a substitute, and only the wealthy had continual access to the real bean. In fact, the term ''bean coffee,'' as opposed to chicory coffee, remained a part of general German vocabulary until well past World War II.

In America, coffee drinking took hold after the Townshend Act of 1767 imposed a tax on tea. This was the fateful tax that set the stage for the Boston Tea Party. America has since been faithful to the bean, to the point where we as a nation drink 45 million cups of the brew each day. However, most of those cups are drunk at home or in the office; until recently, coffeehouses were not commonplace in the United States. But even this is changing as Americans discover that quality coffee has more to offer than just a caffeine kick. It can be a stimulating, sophisticated social diversion which fits right in with the current climate in the United States.

Not to mention that it tastes pretty wonderful, too.

HEALTH FACTS AND MYTHS

Coffee has had a checkered past among health-conscious people. Although first brought to the West as a beverage, once the effects of caffeine were discovered, the coffee debate began. Everyone had a position. Some people considered it a magical liquid that could cure numerous ills. Its virtues are cataloged in one late eighteenth-century manual:

> Virtues of Coffee: Coffee accelerates digestion, corrects crudities, removes colic and flatulencies. It mitigates headaches, cherishes the animal spirits, takes away listlessness and languor, and is serviceable in all obstructions arising from languid circulation. It is a wonderful restorative to emaciated constitutions, and highly refreshing to the studious and sedentary.
>
> The habitual use of coffee would greatly promote sobriety, being in itself a cordial stimulant; it is a most powerful antidote to the temptation of spirituous liquors.
>
> It well could be a welcome beverage to the robust laborer, who would despise a lighter drink.

Of course, just as much has been said as to the contrary, with coffee assuming the blame for everything from ''nervous anxiety, headaches, and twitches'' to impotence in men. Its effects on male virility were described in the 1674

British treatise, "A Women's Petition Against Coffee," mentioned in the preceding chapter. Soon after its publication, England became a tea-drinking nation.

In the name of solving the big coffee debate, King Gustav III of Sweden performed an unusual experiment in the late eighteenth century. Two identical twin brothers were sentenced to death for murder. In the name of science, Gustav commuted their sentence on the condition that throughout their lifetime one brother was to ingest large quantities of tea while the other would drink the same amount of coffee. The tea-drinking brother died first, at the ripe old age of eighty-three and the Swedes have been coffee drinkers ever since.

Coffee does have many beneficial physical effects. It is a stimulant, keeping the mind alert and the body energetic. It is useful during asthma attacks, because the stimulation will aid the body in drying up mucous secretions in the bronchi and will constrict the blood vessels. Caffeine is also chemically similar to theophylline, the drug most commonly prescribed to treat asthma. Additionally, caffeine's ability to constrict blood vessels can also help relieve a painful migraine, as migraine sufferers probably know.

Despite its beneficial effects, popular opinion today casts coffee in a darker role. As perfectly summed up by an herbal tea–sipping woman to her coffee-guzzling companion (I overhead this in a café one Sunday): "Honestly, Jimmy, coffee is a drug." Doctors have taken to recommending that their patients cut down on coffee, and the caffeine in coffee has been shown to be linked to ulcers, not to mention anxiety. Of course, each person reacts to coffee differently. Some people have no problem going directly to sleep after a double espresso, while others are kept awake hours later by their morning café au lait.

However, if you are like me, you will probably be very

surprised to find out that espresso and dark roasted coffee have less caffeine than regular medium-roasted beans. This is because when the beans are roasted to such a dark color, some of the caffeine is burned away. And the gourmet arabica coffee has less than half the caffeine of the ubiquitous robusta strain.

Those who have health concerns about coffee can easily allay their fears by drinking the decaffeinated varieties. The decaffeination process, which is done before the beans are roasted, removes about 96 percent of the caffeine. While decaffeinated coffee will never taste quite as rich as its caffeinated counterpart, companies are striving to develop techniques that will disrupt as little of the physical and chemical structure of the bean as possible. This will help preserve the precious flavor molecules.

At the present writing, there is only one process for decaffeinating coffee beans, but with several variations. Coffee beans are warmed to open their pores and then rinsed with a solvent several times over to remove as much of the caffeine as possible. The coffee is then dried, and the solvent removed.

The solvent of choice for the taste-oriented decaf drinker is methylene chloride (CH_3CL). When this solvent is put directly onto the surface of the bean, the process is known as the "direct method," or the "direct methylene chloride process," of decaffeination. This method preserves more of the coffee flavor than do any of the other methods because it acts only on the caffeine without disturbing anything else in the bean. This leaves virtually all the flavor and aroma intact for you to enjoy without the negative side effects.

A mitigated approach, which also employs methylene chloride as solvent is called the "indirect method," or the "European water process." Do not confuse this with the "Swiss water process," for they are not the same thing.

The indirect method uses plain water initially to rinse the beans of their caffeine. The same water is then mixed with methylene chloride and the caffeine is cleared away. The other coffee components that were dissolved in the water, such as flavor and aroma, are left still floating in the water. This same flavorful water is used to rinse other beans of their caffeine, and soon becomes saturated with very high concentration of flavor molecules. In subsequent rinsing, the water supposedly stops absorbing flavor from the beans and just removes the caffeine.

However tasty methylene chloride decaffeinated coffee may be, concerns about the environmental effects of the chemical may soon cause its disuse. Methylene chloride is now outlawed in most of Europe, which makes the chemical harder to get in the United States. Some scientists now say that methylene chloride may induce cancer in those who ingest it. While the environmental disadvantages of the chemical are not to be disputed, however, the cancer myths are.

Anxiety over methylene chloride stems from its linkage to cancer in laboratory rats. However, the rats did not ingest the chemical as we supposedly might do if we drank it in our decaf. They inhaled it in amounts vaster than any human would ever be exposed to over several lifetimes. Additionally, there is almost no chance of any of the chemical remaining in the bean after you brew your coffee. Methylene chloride vaporizes into oblivion at a temperature of 103 degrees Fahrenheit. Coffee beans are roasted after decaffeination at temperatures close to 400 degrees. The coffee is then brewed at 200 degrees before you drink it. The likelihood of any trace of methylene chloride clinging to your bean should not worry you.

The environmental dangers are not so easily put aside as the health fears, for it has been shown that methylene chloride poses hazards to the ozone layer. Even if the United States does not follow Europe's example by banning its use entirely, however, other chemicals are now moving to replace it, and worldwide discontinuation will serve as a de facto global ban.

An environmentally friendly and healthy way to decaffeinate beans is the Swiss water process in which water alone is used to dissolve the caffeine from the bean. Although the beans still suffer from lack of flavor, the Coffex Company, which was responsible for the method, is working hard to improve the quality of the beans it decaffeinates.

Some other promising methods are being developed. One of them, called the "natural process," uses carbon dioxide to decaffeinate the beans, while another uses ethyl acetate. Keep a lookout for these and other new developments when you buy decaffeinated coffee. If you are not sure what type of method is used on the beans you buy, ask your coffee merchant. If he or she does not know, think about switching to a merchant who is better informed about the products he or she sells.

THE VOCABULARY OF
THE COFFEE
CONNOISSEUR

If you are serious about coffee consumption, you will find it helpful to develop the necessary vocabulary. Here are some of the words that are frequently used in discussing coffee.

Acidity: The sharp, bracing quality that balances out the richer, heavier coffee components. Acidity in coffee should be a pleasant, crisp sensation, comparable to the acidity in a well-balanced glass of wine.

Aroma: The luscious, wake-me-up smell emanating from your freshly roasted beans. The aroma in coffee beans is liberated during several stages of its journey from green seed to rich beverage. Roasting brings out the majority of the essential oils, which produce the aroma. Grinding the beans will release even more of the beans' scent, and the hot water will release the last essence of fragrance left in the bean. Inhale all along the way and eventually you will be able to train your nose to discern different roasts as they metamorphose into your morning cup.

Body: The feeling of the brew in your mouth, how heavily it sits on your tongue, and how completely it surrounds and coats your mouth. The heaviness or lightness of a particular cup results from many factors in its making, including how long the beans were roasted, how much water was used during brewing, and what percentage of the beans' oils are allowed to enter your cup. The correct body of a drink is strictly a matter of preference, but generally speaking, coffee is once again comparable to wine: its weight should be heavy enough that it resonates for a few seconds after you swallow but not so thick that it feels oily as it slides down your throat.

Flavor: A combination of taste, aroma, body, and acidity. Professional tasters use many words to describe the flavor of coffee: woody, earthy, turpentiny, fruity, sweet, spicy, harsh, soft, and so on. There is no one ultimate flavor that all coffees aspire toward, as each bean has its own distinct characteristics that either attract, repel, or merely bore the taster. Taste is perhaps the most personal matter in all of coffee discernment.

A CONNOISSEUR'S GUIDE TO THE BEAN

Understanding and appreciating all the many coffee varieties that are now available can be a daunting task. Varieties of coffee beans vary as much as do varieties of any other living thing, but they do share some similar qualities. All coffee beans share certain basic characteristics, but they differ from one another in some ways. As Timothy Castle points out in his book, *The Perfect Cup,* all beans ''bring with them the smell of the forests they grew near, the taste of the water that soaked their roots, the flavors of the fruits that grew near them.''

However unique the beans from each coffee plantation and from every passing year may be, here is a list of what you can expect of the types of coffee produced in various countries.

COFFEE-PRODUCING COUNTRIES:

Brazil: Coffee producers in Brazil, one of the world's largest coffee producers, are currently more interested in quantity than in quality. Although most of the crop is arabica beans, they are not processed carefully enough to compete with coffees from the more exacting growers in other parts of the world. At its best, Brazil's coffee is spicy and bright. At its worst, it is manufactured into canned and instant coffee.

Margogipe coffee hails from the tiny Brazilian village for which it is named, where a regular coffee plant somehow mutated to produce extra-large beans. Cuttings of this mutation were introduced into Guatemala and Mexico, and now several countries produce this acidic, snappy bean. It benefits from a medium roast, which heightens its clear, bold flavor.

Colombia: Colombian coffee, now synonymous with Juan Valdez and his troop of hand-pickers, runs just behind Brazil in the size of its coffee production. Colombian coffees make a very dependable, rich brew with a pleasing hint of sweetness. They are best drunk unblended, although an expert can mellow a more sour blend. Colombia separates its coffee into two bean sizes—supremos, which are large, and excelsos, which are not. However, as of now, the difference is not standardized, and one estate's supremo may be smaller than another's excelso. The flavor of the two also varies from grower to grower and therefore will be inconsistent in different coffee shops.

Costa Rica: Costa Rican coffees are another very dependable bet for a consistently good, well-balanced cup. They tend to be rich, dark, winy-flavored beans with a nice snappy aftertaste. The beans themselves are small but uniform in size and shape.

Cuba: Not known for its intense flavor, the Cuban bean is usually roasted dark for espresso. The quality of the bean, therefore, depends largely on the roaster rather than the grower. Most Cuban coffee is sold to Japan rather than to the United States, so you are unlikely to find it at your local coffee shop.

Dominican Republic: A bland all-purpose coffee that is sold mostly to the United States. Unless the price is right, you will do better to try something else.

Ecuador: Although the climate and high altitude in Ecuador deliver a fine environment for coffee, the beans have not yet met their potential. Ecuadorian coffees are used mostly in blends and are rarely sold by themselves.

El Salvador: El Salvador produces a pleasantly unusual high-grown bean that is favored for espresso roasts. The rest of its substantial coffee export is sold for blends and for canned coffee. Not much of this canned coffee reaches the United States.

Ethiopia: In the supposed birthplace of the bean, coffee is still harvested for the most part from wild trees. The resulting flavor is earthy, sometimes leaning toward vegetal, though at best winy and woodsy. Genuine Ethiopian Harrar, named for its place of origin, is dependably viscous, spicy, and fruity. Unfortunately it is also quite expensive, and frequently what is sold as Harrar is merely a pale impostor. If you buy your Harrar from a scrupulous dealer, however, you will be in for a very special coffee experience.

Like Colombian excelsos and supremos, Ethiopian Harrar beans are divided into longberries and shortberries depending on their size. There is no clear difference in flavor.

Guatemala: Smoky and well-balanced, Guatemalan coffee—from the areas surrounding Coban, Antigua, Atitlan, and Feihanes—produces one of the world's best, most distinctive cups. This is a coffee you must try at least once.

Haiti: Espresso-drinking Europeans favor the soft brown Haitian bean for its sugary undertones and mellow flavor. It is particularly good for dark roasting, as it does not become too bitter. The high-grown varieties are better than the low-grown coffees, which can be muddy.

U.S.A.—Hawaii: Hawaii is the only state in the United States that consistently produces good coffee beans. The most renowned coffee-growing region of the Hawaiian islands is undoubtedly Kona, famous for its soft, fragrant beans. Since Kona coffee is quite pricey, buy just a small amount to taste. Many people feel it does not live up to its price class.

Honduras: Not a major competitor in the coffee market, Honduras produces unremarkable blend-type coffees with a mild flavor that can be a bit sour.

India: India entered the coffee competition rather late, after being committed only to tea for many years. But do not let this stop you from appreciating an aged monsoon Malabar with its intense, lingering flavor and rich texture, or savoring a delightful cup of Mysore, with a gentle perfumed flavor and a velvety body.

Indonesia: Some of the world's most desirable coffees come from the remote islands of Indonesia where the Dutch planted a scant few seedlings close to three hundred years ago. Java coffee is probably the best known; the word "Java" is sometimes used instead of "coffee." Although full-bodied, chocolaty Java tastes fine on its own, it has always benefited from blending with the lighter, brighter mocha. Other regions of Indonesia include Sumatra, which produces a woodsy, creamy brew, and Celebes, which produces a spicy coffee.

Jamaica: Although Jamaican Blue Mountain coffee used to be one of the most prestigious and expensive coffees in the world, today it is just expensive. Unfortunately the fragrant, nutty coffee of the past has been corrupted, and the name ''Blue Mountain'' or ''Jamaican High-Grown'' can now refer to almost any of the inferior beans that grow on the island. The cream of the Jamaican crop is exported to the high-paying Japanese, leaving very little coffee of quality for the United States.

Kenya: Kenyan coffee delivers a winy, flowery flavor and rich texture that is sought after worldwide. Kenyan peaberries are small round beans that are ideal for home roasters because they roll easily around the pan, producing an even roast. The poorer quality Kenyans may taste a bit harsh, however.

Malawi: Although Malawi produces a small crop, it is composed solely of high-grade arabica beans that are reminiscent of Kenyan varieties, with added body and wilder nuances.

Mexico: Mexico produces a popular blender coffee that is also quite pleasing on its own. It has a woodsy, rich aroma, a delicate body, and a mellow, satisfying flavor. The beans tend to be rather large, making them an attractive choice for display or for coating in chocolate.

Nicaragua: Another popular blender coffee comes from Nicaragua. These beans make a mildly flavored acidic cup with a medium body, which some people compare to Guatemalan coffee, sans the smoky aftertaste. Nicaraguan beans are rarely found sold by themselves in shops.

Panama: Because Panama produces a limited quantity of very unusual coffee, Panamanian beans are scarce in the United States. If you happen to come across them, do sample some, and be rewarded with a clean, creamy, sweet morning cup.

Papua New Guinea: Beans grown in Papua New Guinea have what some people consider a perfect body, and they make for an engaging, lively brew. It tastes the way one imagines good coffee to taste: purely of itself. They seem to grow in popularity as they become better known on the market.

Peru: Peruvian coffees are very inconsistent, due in part to the constant political upheavals that plague the country. Some of the high-grown beans are superbly mild and sweet, with good body and acidity. However, some of Peru's coffee can make you want to switch to tea. If the political situation ever stabilizes in Peru, the overall quality of the coffee is likely to improve.

Tanzania: This high-grown coffee is what mountain coffee is all about: rich, smooth, and tempting. Some of the best Tanzanian coffee is grown on the slopes of Mount Kilimanjaro.

Venezuela: Venezuelan coffee is also sometimes known as Maracaibo, for the port it is sent from. It is also occasionally called Táchiras. They range in quality from delicate, silky brews with fine acidity and a sweet flavor, to murky, muddy mixtures best avoided. Due to the increased activity in the oil industry, Venezuela produces less and less coffee every year.

Yemen: Yemen Mochas fall into the familiar category of a legend not living up to its reputation. Historically, they have always been blended with Java coffee to produce an even-bodied, sprightly brew. On its own, the finest Mocha coffee is rich, fruity, and spicy with a pleasant sharpness that mixes well with heavier-bodied coffees. Buy your Mocha from a reputable dealer, or you might end up with counterfeit beans worth very little in the cup.

Zaire: Most coffee from Zaire is the mediocre robusta variety that is of little interest to the true connoisseur. The bulk of its exports are processed into canned and instant coffee. There are two regions presently growing arabica beans in mountainous conditions. The result is a wonderful balance of flavor, acidity, and body. Buy these beans if you can find them.

Zimbabwe: A minor producer of thick, winy coffee beans that are reminiscent of Kenyan beans. They are rarely seen in the United States.

GROWING AND PROCESSING THE BEAN

Although understanding the coffee bean's journey from seedling to beverage may not directly further your enjoyment of the brew, understanding the link between the gleaming brown beans you buy in gourmet markets and the yellowish-green seeds of a fragrant berry bush will help you appreciate just how far those beans have come.

The coffee shrub—or tree, as it is sometimes called—most likely originated in Africa, specifically Ethiopia, although it may also be indigenous to Yemen, on the Arabian Peninsula. Since then it has been transported to warm climates all over the globe, as far away as South America and Indonesia. As mentioned earlier, coffee plants for commercial cultivation are divided into two principle species: the arabica plant and the robusta. The robusta, as its name suggests, is the heartier of the two. It can grow in varying conditions which great success, unlike the finicky arabica, which needs optimal growing conditions to produce its crop. The robusta beans are bigger and browner than their pale green cousins, however, the better flavor is contained in these greenish seeds, making arabica beans the choice for more serious, quality-minded buyers. The robusta beans are used mainly in lower-grade coffee—for example, the canned stuff on your supermarket shelves—and for instant coffee granules.

The ideal climate for coffee trees can be simply summed up, as Timothy Castle has done: coffee trees are comfortable anywhere that people are. This means an average temperature of between 20°C. and 26°C., (68°F to 79°F.) with the arabicas needing the more moderate temperatures and the robustas doing well in the higher temperature zone. You will have probably noticed the prevalence of coffee beans labeled "mountain grown" or "high-grown." This is because the better coffees, including the finest of the arabicas, are grown at high altitudes while robustas can tolerate the lower altitudes. Medium rainfall, medium humidity, and a mixture of sun and shade will all contribute to happy fruit-bearing plants.

Most coffee plants are grown on vast plantations—or estates, as they are sometimes called—where they are constantly pruned so that they remain small (under 9 feet), which facilitates harvesting. The trees develop perfumed white flowers that eventually give way to sweet red berries called coffee cherries. These cherries contain the coffee beans, which are the seeds of the coffee tree. The coffee cherries ripen individually like any other fruit, and this is why Juan Valdez makes such a point of rounding up the finest team of hand-pickers who make sure not to pick any bean before its time. Each coffee tree is then harvested several times as the cherries ripen from hard green nodules to fleshy scarlet fruits.

On some less discriminating estates, the coffee cherries are strip-picked. Instead of carefully plucking each ripe bean from the branch, the strip-pickers run their hands or a tool along the whole branch, stripping it of everything, including fruit, leaves, and twigs. The ripe cherries are then separated out for commercial processing, and the rest is discarded. Any fruit that is not perfectly ripe is of no use to the plantation. Underripe fruit results in beans that have not had time to develop their characteristic flavor, and over-ripening leads to cherries whose skin has burst or cracked, attracting mold, fungus, and disease.

Two methods are currently employed to separate the bean from the cherry after the fruit is laboriously gathered. In the "wet" method, or "washed" coffee, whole coffee cherries are fed into a machine, which scrapes the bean away from the fruit. The mixture of beans and fruit is then soaked in tanks of water where the buoyant fruit floats to the top and is later lifted off while the heavier, denser beans sink to the bottom. The beans are left in the water to soak for several days to undergo a slight fermentation process that can help increase the perceptible acidity in the beverage. This—plus the added fact that washed beans are handled quite frequently, giving the growers many chances to weed out the defective beans—causes washed beans to be considered generally of a higher quality than unwashed.

In the dry method of separating the coffee cherries from the beans, the cherries are dried on long concrete blocks in the sun. When the fruit shrivels and dries up, its flesh is separated from the bean by mechanical means. The coffee does not come into contact with any water, and so its acidity level is not affected. However, beans that have been dry-processed will sometimes produce a beverage with more earthiness and a better, richer body.

Unfortunately, some estates now dry their coffee in large steel drums. While this results in a faster drying time and quicker profits, the coffee does not develop the characteristic flavor of sun-dried beans, which in the end leaves no advantage to this process other than water conservation and convenience.

Once the beans have been separated from the cherries, the next step is removing the thin, papery husk that surrounds each bean. Expensive high-tech decorticating machines are needed to accomplish this task. Most individual growers do not own one of these machines, so they send their beans to processing centers run by a plantation co-operative. There the parchments are polished off the beans, and machines are used to grade and sort the beans according to size and type. This sorting step is very important for the roasters, who need to know that the beans they have purchased are all the same size so that they will roast evenly.

The sorting machine has an electronic eye that rejects the beans which just don't fit in. It can account for weight, size, and color, and it separates the beans into many different grades. After they are mechanically graded, laborers then go over the beans to make sure they were graded accurately.

By the time they get to the importer and the roaster, the beans are all ready to be roasted and distributed. Unroasted green beans, however, can last for several months or even years without any deterioration in quality. Of course, this is possible only if the coffee is stored under optimal conditions, and in the hot and humid climates where most coffee is grown, this is rarely the case. Instead, burlap sacks of coffee beans are stored in dirt-floored warehouses close to the docks, waiting to be exported. In conditions like these, the beans are left vulnerable to molds and fungi, which will destroy their precious flavor. This is another reason to choose a reliable roaster who is knowledgeable enough to reject contaminated beans and savvy enough to accept only beans that were milled within ten days of export.

Now that you have followed the coffee bean's journey halfway around the world, through many different procedures and people, I am sure that your morning cup will seem all the richer for it.

ROASTING AND BLENDING

It is hard to imagine anyone drinking a beverage made from the green, unroasted beans of the coffee tree. While these beans have the potential to make a great cup of coffee, that potential is not unlocked until the green beans are roasted to at least a pale brown, and the flavor will become more pronounced as the beans darken to a deeper hue. Roasting brings out the personality of a bean and helps to develop the mineral salts, sugars, aromatic oils, and starches that account for flavor and aroma in your cup.

When the bean is roasted, it undergoes several physical changes. First it loses 15 to 20 percent of its body weight, mostly due to water evaporation. However, although the bean loses weight, it increases in volume as the internal gases expand under the heat and cause the bean to swell. The structure of the bean also changes; it becomes brittle, making it easy to grind. The deep brown color comes in stages as the beans are roasted. Some beans are roasted until they are black, so that their volatile oils rise to the surface in tiny beads. This is what espresso beans look like.

Bitterness in coffee can be traced to the temperature at which the coffee was roasted—the higher the temperature, the more bitter the brew. However, bitterness is not always frowned upon in the coffee trade. Many people around the globe prefer bitter coffee, and bitterness is a common feature in most espressos. It is, however, an aquired taste.

The roaster who prepares the beans must decide which roasting style is most suited to each variety of bean. Roasted coffee beans come in several shades of darkness, from the palest cinnamon color preferred by the Americans and the British to the deepest chocolate brown. To add to the confusion, there are no set standards for the roasters to follow, and no universally accepted terminology for the levels of roasting. Therefore, a lightly roasted bean might go by several names in different parts of the country, being called cinnamon roast on the east coast and half-city roast on the west coast.

Here is a synopsis of each type of roast and the various names under which each type can be found.

Light Roast: Also known as a cinnamon roast or a half-city roast, these beans are a pale reddish brown and will produce a light-bodied, somewhat bland brew. This is the roast that all commercial and canned coffees use. Most true coffee lovers do not feel that this roast extracts enough flavor from the bean, and quality coffee roasters never stop here when roasting a batch.

Medium Roast: Also called city, American, regular, and breakfast roast, these beans are a bit deeper in color than the light roasts, but not yet as intense as they could be. This is the best style for some of the more subtle bean varieties whose flavor would be completely burned away by a higher roast. Medium-roast coffees are preferred for breakfast by many people and are usually drunk with milk and sugar. This is an all-purpose roast favored by most Americans and is considered the standard in this country among better quality commercial roasters. If you prefer a darker roast, you will have to seek it out in coffee specialty shops.

Dark Roast: There are two types of dark roasts before you reach the darkest of all: the espresso roast. The lighter of the two is called full-city, high, or Vienna roast, and occurs when the oil from the beans just begins to hit the surface. The color will be a deep sienna with a slight sheen from the oil. This is the favorite roast of many smaller quality-oriented coffee merchants who consider it the perfect balance between acidity and bitterness. The brew will have a full, syrupy texture, a deep color, and a rich flavor. It is often used for making espresso and espresso drinks by people who favor it over a darker espresso roast. This roast brings out the best in most beans, but can obscure the more delicate types, which benefit from a medium roast.

A lot of confusion in the coffee trade arises over the difference between the lighter roast and one shade darker. Every roaster has a different idea of what defines a ''dark roast'' and one manufacturer's high roast might be lighter than another's French or Continental roast. If all things were equal, the French or Continental roast would be just a tad darker than the high roast, with a bit more surface oil and a richer hue. However, at this point it is very easy to cross the border into an espresso roast, which is the next level of roasting.

Espresso Roast: Also known as Italian roast, these beans are nearly black and very shiny from the oils. There is a very thin line between these beans and overroasted, burned beans. In fact, many people regard these beans as burned beans and prefer to use the French or Vienna roasts for their espresso. Italian roasts produce a very bitter, creamy brew, which some people adore. However, many of the varietal characteristics of the beans will be muddied by the intensity of the roasting process. It is for this reason that many unscrupulous dealers use poorer quality beans for an espresso roast, figuring that at that level of roasting no one will be able to taste the defects. Unfortunately, this is sometimes the case.

One note for the caffeine sensitive: the darker the bean is roasted, the less caffeine it will contain. Some of the caffeine will burn off while the bean is roasting for such a long period of time and at such high temperatures (up to 430°F.). On average, espresso coffee has about half as much caffeine as a cup made from medium-roasted beans.

BUYING AND STORING
THE BEANS

The most important thing you can do for your brew is to find a reliable coffee source. This means a dealer who sells *fresh* roasted beans. Luckily, with the increase in the number of well-informed coffee drinkers, quality coffee merchants are popping up around big cities like dandelions in a lawn. Of course, the best place to buy beans would be directly from the roaster. You can be guaranteed freshness by seeing the giant coffee roaster spit out your beans, which are immediately bagged for you to take home, although coffee roasted that morning will certainly do.

Since most of us are not lucky enough to live near a coffee roaster, the next best thing is to find a reliable merchant. The ideal coffee seller buys only a small amount of the very best coffee at a time and disposes of beans that are more than a week or two old. One New York merchant, for example, donates his week-old beans to a city food harvest program. If you wish to buy good coffee, you must be able to trust the people you are buying it from. Make sure that the coffees are clearly labeled, and that the counter people are knowledgeable. They should know where and how long ago the coffee was roasted and what method of decaffeination was used if you buy decaffeinated beans.

Another way to tell the quality of a retailer is to try the house blend. Coffee merchants truly involved with their beans will be proud of their own blends, which should reflect and enhance the subtle nuances of each variety.

Once you have selected your beans and brought them home (never, ever buy ground beans), the next task is storing them properly to preserve their freshness. There are many opinions on how this is best accomplished, but when you look at the causes of bean staling, the best solutions become clearer.

The foremost element that will stale your beans is air. Every time the beans are exposed to the atmosphere they will lose some of the volatile oils that translate into flavor and aroma in the cup. The next nemesis is moisture, which will also speed up bean deterioration. So the optimal environment for your beans is a dry vacuum.

To achieve the vacuum, you will have to store the beans in an airtight container. Special coffee containers with airtight lids are available, and they serve very well to keep the beans fresh. You can store your coffee in one of these on your countertop for up to a week without much loss of flavor. A Mason jar with a sealed lid works well also. Just avoid plastic, which will absorb the coffee's odor and oils and could become rancid if not cleaned often. Another thing to keep in mind is that every time you open the jar, air will leak in, so close it quickly after measuring out your beans.

A popular but ineffective way to store fresh beans is in the refrigerator in the bag that the beans were packed in at the shop. This will result in stale coffee. The bags that your merchant scoops the coffee into are not meant for storage. Although they may be wax-coated, they are not airtight. Furthermore, when coffee is stored in the refrigerator, moist air will condense on your beans. This will stale your coffee before than you can drink it, robbing you of the rich flavor and intense aroma the beans had when your first bought them.

Some people swear by freezing the beans after sealing them in airtight containers (Ziploc freezer bags are good for this). The beans are then ground while still frozen. This technique will keep your beans relatively fresh for up to three months, but don't try to store them beyond that. Also, remember that every time you open and close your freezer, moisture will condense on the beans. Try to store them in the back of a rarely used freezer, if you have such a thing.

Although these precautions may seem burdensome, they are really quite simple once you set up a system for buying and storing. And the payoff for your efforts is mighty impressive.

GRINDING

Next to the freshness of the coffee beans, the second most important concern of coffee connoisseurs is the freshness of the coffee grinds. Grinding whole beans just moments before brewing will produce the most flavorful cup, for as soon as the beans are ground, the essential oils trapped inside them will begin to evaporate, and take the coffee flavor with them! Electric coffee grinders are now easily available and inexpensive, and purchasing one is a small investment to make for such flavorful rewards.

When grinding your beans, keep in mind the correct size of the grind you will need for your brewing method. Coarse grinds are seldom used by coffee mavens because the brewing methods to which they are suited do not produce the best flavor. Percolators, boiling, and the coffee sock all require a coarse grind, which resembles cake crumbs in size. A medium or medium-fine grind will have the texture of fine sand or cornmeal. It is the most popular and versatile grind, and is used for the electric drip machine, the Melitta filter drip, the press pot, and the Neapolitan flip-drip. Lastly, the finest grind feels almost powdery. It is best suited for making espresso, Turkish coffee, or brewing regular coffee in a vacuum pot.

BREWING

Ever since coffee came into favor as a drink, people have been trying to figure out the best ways to extract the unique flavor from the bean. There are many methods of doing this, including several tried and true ways that will guarantee a good cup and dozens of other ways that serve as examples of what not to do.

But be warned—there is no definitive way to brew a perfect cup, because there is no such thing. Perfection for me may be mere colored water for you, and one person's prized formula is probably someone else's mud. I will offer several ways of making a good cup of coffee. They all have some general points in common, the most important of which is using the finest, freshest beans you can find. After that, you will need to use trial and error to determine your favorite way of making coffee.

GENERAL TIPS FOR COFFEE MAKING

The little things always really do make the difference, and here is a list of several seemingly petty details that will make the difference between a memorable morning cup and a merely mediocre one.

Always use cold fresh water. Hot water will have been sitting in the pipes longer and has probably acquired a metallic taste. It has also lost all of the oxygen necessary in water to brew a good cup. Let the cold water run for a few seconds to get the freshest water, and then proceed. If your water does not taste good straight from the tap, it is not going to be good enough to brew with. You might consider using spring water. Some people will think you are being fanatical, but do not listen to them. They probably drink instant.

Use the correct amount of coffee per cup: one coffee measure (two tablespoons) to a six-ounce cup. Note that most mugs hold eight ounces of liquid, so if you drink from a mug, use three tablespoons of coffee.

The size of the grind is very important in achieving the best flavor. Use the right size grind for whatever method of brewing you choose. For a fuller discussion, see the section on grinding.

Make sure your equipment is clean. Coffee contains oils that can turn rancid and impart an unpleasant aftertaste to your drink. Thoroughly wash your coffee utensils after every use.

Drink the coffee as soon as it is made; cold coffee is an insult to your carefully picked, fresh-roasted beans. I have never found a way to reheat coffee successfully (although some people use a microwave), so get it while it's hot. If you must store brewed coffee for a short period of time, use one of those nice thermos flasks that are now available. In some of the newer automatic coffee makers the coffee drips directly into a thermos, which is a marked improvement over the hot plate on which glass coffee pots usually sit. Coffee that sits too long on a hot plate will turn so dark and bitter that no amount of cream and sugar will lighten it.

Here is a trick I have learned to help keep your brew hotter longer: rinse out your pot and your mug with hot water before filling it with coffee. This tip is a vestige from my tea days, where it was de rigueur. A tea cozy works pretty well on a coffee pot too.

COFFEE-MAKING EQUIPMENT AND TECHNIQUES

Boiling

In the nascent years of coffee making, boiling was the only way people knew of to make the drink. The exact method of boiling changed with time and fashion: boiling times were lengthened and shortened; flavorings were added and subtracted; new techniques were developed for separating the hated grounds from the liquid. One early American recipe calls for a boiling time of thirty minutes and recommends the use of a piece of fish skin to settle the grounds.

A slightly later one from the American West directs the brewer to mix a whole egg, shell and all, with the grounds before boiling it all in water for three to four hours. The grounds are supposed to congeal with the egg white while the shell clarifies the liquid and the yolk adds richness to the drink. The original recipe called for twelve gallons of water and sixteen pounds of coffee, which would have made enough coffee to feed the family and farmhands for a week, reheating as needed. It was customary never to wash the coffee pot so as not to lose the potency built up over generations.

Just out of curiosity, I tried both these methods—although I had to use a clean pot—and found them as awful as you can imagine. It is a wonder that so many people still loved coffee even after such hostile treatment as this.

Lucky for us, boiled coffee has lost most of its cache. Today, boiling is reserved for camping trips and for Turkish coffee, which has its own special etiquette. Boiled coffee tends to taste more bitter than other types of coffee, because the boiling water extracts from the bean certain astringent elements that are not soluble by other means. That is why a water temperature just under boiling is recommended for smooth coffee.

If you would like to make boiled coffee, for each cup of water place one tablespoon coarsely ground coffee into a pot and stir well. Bring the water to a gentle boil and immediately remove the pot from the heat. Let the mixture infuse for five to ten more minutes.

As for the grounds, there are better ways than fish skin to eliminate these. One is to let the coffee sit for a moment or two after it is boiled. The grounds will sink to the bottom of the pot, and the liquid can be carefully poured off. A drop of cold water added to the pot just after boiling will accelerate the settling process. Straining the coffee through cheesecloth also works wells, but who brings cheesecloth on a camping trip?

Percolator

Ah, the smell and sound of coffee perking away in a stainless-steel pot. No other smell is more comforting and delicious than this. It conjures up scenes of sunshine-filled mornings in the suburbs, bacon and eggs, and the newspaper, complete with funnies. Nothing else captures memories waking up like the percolator does.

But then there's the taste, or lack of it. As anyone who's ever had a cold knows, flavor and aroma are inseparable. If your nose is too congested for you to smell, all food loses its flavor. So, while the aroma of your morning cup is as important as the flavor, understand that the aroma *is* the flavor. And that terrific scent wafting up the stairway to your bedroom contains many of the precious flavor molecules. The resulting brew tastes (if it tastes at all) bitter, lifeless, and dull.

The percolator consists of a metal pot with a central hollow core connected to a filter basket holding coarsely ground coffee. Boiling water is circulated over and over again through the tube and past the grounds until a dark liquor is produced. Less coffee is needed in this method, since the water passes through it many times and more flavor can be extracted. However, the boiling water also extracts the bean's bitterness.

If you happen to have a relic percolator and desperately want to use it, here are directions:

1. Fill the filter basket with the appropriate amount of coarsely ground coffee: one measure (two tablespoons) for each six-ounce cup.
2. Add cold water to the pot and replace filter basket.
3. Plug the pot in and let the coffee bubble and boil for about five minutes.
4. Breathe deep. Savor the aroma. Reminisce.
5. Pour the fresh coffee down the sink and drink the stuff you were simultaneously brewing in your Mr. Coffee.
6. Realize you have the best of both worlds.

Brought on the scene in 1825, the percolator was for many years the most popular method of brewing coffee in America. Luckily, as people begin to experience coffee made other ways, this is changing for the better.

Drip

The drip method is used in the automatic drip coffee makers (Mr. Coffee and clones), the Melitta filter, and the

Swiss gold filter cone. It is increasingly becoming the most popular way to brew coffee in America today, and it produces wonderful results, especially given the small amount of effort and expense that goes into each cup. Finely ground coffee is placed in a filter cup and near-boiling water is poured over the grounds. The hot water extracts the flavor and drips down into the pot, leaving the messy grinds behind. The flavor is smooth and mellow because the bitter elements are not overextracted, as they are in boiled coffee.

Seeing that the water comes into contact with the coffee grounds for only a short time, they need to be finer than for boiled or perked coffee, but not powdery, as for Turkish. If the grounds are too coarse, the coffee will not be strong enough. If they are too fine, they will drip though the filter and result in a cloudy cup.

There are many types of filter pots on the market. The automatic drip pots offer a convenient way to make a large amount of coffee quickly. They also heat the water to the correct temperature so you are guaranteed a smooth cup if you measure carefully. Some work on a timer system. A friend of mine keeps her coffee machine on the nightstand next to her bed. She sets it on a timer and wakes up every morning to steaming coffee within arm's reach.

The Melitta filter system was an innovation of an early twentieth-century German woman named Melitta Bentz. Legend says that she used to filter her coffee through a linen towel, and one day thought to use blotter paper instead. Paper filters are very convenient for disposing of the grounds, but they do have the major environmental disadvantage of being bleached with chlorine. Unbleached filters are now available, but people have complained that they impart a distinct cardboard flavor to the coffee. I like to use a gold filter cone, which is inexpensive compared to the amount of money you will spend over the years buying paper filters. The gold filter kills no trees, leaves no after-taste, and is made to last forever—something rare in this age of disposable products. It costs about $15.00 and is widely available at coffee specialty stores.

Another advantage of the gold filter is that it allows more of the coffee oils to pass through to your cup, adding body to your brew, whereas paper filters absorb most of this oil.

To make coffee using the filter method, measure two to three rounded tablespoons of medium-ground coffee per cup into a filter-lined cone poised over your pot or cup. Heat cold fresh water just until it boils. Remove the water from the heat and let it cool for a few moments so it reaches about 200°F. First add just a few splashes of the water to the coffee grounds to moisten them slightly. Let them ab-sorb all of that water before pouring on the rest. This will help to prevent the water from going through the grounds too quickly without extracting maximum flavor, as would happen if you dumped all the water onto the grounds at once. If you rinse the pot or mug out with hot water before you make the coffee, the drink will remain hot longer.

Press Pot

The press pot method is popular with people who enjoy coffee with more body than is usually produced by the filter drip method, even with the filter cone. The brew has a voluptuous texture without the bitterness of an espresso. It is best drunk black, though sugar is fine if you like it sweet.

The French press pot was introduced in the early 1920's, and is very sleek and elegant in its design. The coffee brews by infusion, in much the same way as do tea leaves (in fact, you may use your press pot to make tea as well). Hot water is poured over the coffee and allowed to steep for five minutes. Then the filter is plunged down to the bottom, catching all of the coffee grounds. Medium-ground coffee works best; the finer grinds clog up the filter, making it difficult to work the plunger down. The resultant coffee is heady and clear. If the brew tastes stronger than what you are used to, it might be because the grounds remaining at the bottom of the pot continue to steep and flavor the liquid, albeit not very much. Also, the metal filter allows all of the coffee oils to pass through unhindered—unlike a paper filter, which absorbs them—and they will add depth and flavor as well as body to your cup.

To brew, place two tablespoons fresh roasted medium-grind coffee per cup in the glass pot, and add the right amount of just-under-boiling water (bring the kettle to a full boil, remove it from heat, and let it sit for a few moments before you pour). Stir it all up, and then let it steep for four to five minutes. Press the plunger down, and serve the coffee at once. If you need to keep the coffee warm for a bit, either transfer it to a thermos or scald the pot with boiling water before you begin your brew and cover with a tea cozy while it steeps.

Neapolitan Flip-Drip

I just adore the name of this contraption, which I had never heard of until I started writing this book. I had always called this pot the "Italian machinetta" or the "café filtre" as it is known in France. Both names are acceptable for this method but no where nearly as amusing as the flip-drip—its American name, which perfectly describes the process employed for brewing.

The pot itself looks as if it doesn't know which way is up. When set on the stove to boil, the spout points down as if the coffee will pour out onto your floor. But in fact the water never reaches that portion of the pot until you flip it over, and then the spout will point in the correct direction for neat pouring.

To make your coffee in the flip-drip, fill the bottom half of the pot with fresh cold water. Place medium-fine-ground coffee in the enclosed filter basket and twist on the upper portion. When the water begins to boil, you will notice steam escaping from the hole situated just below the filter basket. At this point, remove the pot from the heat and flip it over. The hot water will pass through the grounds in the filter and end up as rich, thick coffee in what is now the bottom half. Simply serve directly from the pot. Make sure to serve it quickly because most flip-drips are made of aluminum, which does not retain heat. The aluminum also tends to taste metallic and needs vigorous cleaning after each use. However, the coffee is as rich as it comes.

Coffee Sock

During my years as a tea drinker, I used a coffee sock to brew tea when I was only making one cup. A coffee sock is exactly what one would picture from its name: a sock-shaped piece of cloth that is filled with ground coffee beans and immersed in near-boiling water. Although it worked pretty well for tea, I gave it up upon the insistence of all my friends, who referred to my method as the ''dirty sock'' way of making tea. It was rather dingy looking after so many soakings in brown tea.

I came back to the sock (a new, clean one) when I started drinking coffee. After reading a report on the ecological ramifications of coffee filters, I thought I would do my part to save the environment. For all my good intentions and effort, I have never been able to produce a superior cup of coffee using the sock method, so I do not have much advice for you. The sock seemed either too thick, which produces thin coffee because too much of the oil was absorbed, or too thin, which made a muddy cup.

Also, the sock needs to be cleaned very well or the cloth will absorb bitter, oily coffee residue, which can build up and seep into your cup. Some people swear by this method, though, and the sock is ecologically sound. If it interests you or if you get one as a gift from a friend who knows you love coffee but does not love it herself, try it and see. Let me know if you have better luck than I. You can always use it for tea.

Vacuum Pot

Another innovation from the elusive days of the leisured classes, the vacuum pot is terrific if you have plenty of time to kill and a penchant for theatrics. Developed in 1840 by a marine scientist named Robert Napier, it has all but disappeared from the dinner tables of today. Although the coffee is clear and the method seductive, it take a very long time to brew, makes a lot of noise while doing so, and is messy to clean. All in all, it's not a practical way to make coffee in today's busy climate.

Every coffee enthusiast should use the vacuum pot at least once, because it really is fascinating and beautiful to watch. The pot is composed of two glass globes, one fitting on top of the other and sealed together to create a vacuum. Between the bowls hangs a funnel cone with a filter, which is attached to the upper chamber before brewing. Water is placed in the lower globe and heated very slowly over a lamp. When it vaporizes, it rises into the upper globe where the coffee grounds are. Then the heat is turned off, and as the liquid cools, with a mighty suck and slurp, it is drawn back down to the lower pot through the filter, metamorphosing into smooth and fragrant coffee. Children will be in awe of this presentation.

To make coffee in a vacuum pot, fill the bottom bowl with fresh cold water. Attach the filter and funnel to the top bowl and place it over the bottom one, twisting the two together to create the necessary seal. Place the proper amount of finely ground coffee in the upper beaker. When the water from the lower chamber bubbles over the ground coffee in the upper part, stir them well and then wait. The coffee will drip back into the lower bowl. Just separate the two bowls and serve.

The Ibrit: Turkish Coffee

Making Turkish coffee in its classic form requires a ritual akin to the Japanese tea ceremony. If you were a guest in the home of a very wealthy nineteenth-century Turkish host, your coffee would probably be roasted right in front of you over the fire. A servant would select the plumpest green beans from a mound and roast them in a cast-iron pot until they turned the perfect chocolate-brown color, the aroma whetting the appetites of everyone present. Then the servant would grind the beans in a tall, decorative brass hand grinder (these grinders, incidentally, are still used in very traditional homes and restaurants) until they were powdery-fine. Fresh water would be drawn and put into a small brass cone-shaped pot called an *ibrit*. Then sugar and spices, perhaps cardamom or cloves, would be stirred in. The coffee would be added next and the whole mixture very gently brought just to boil and immediately removed from the heat. This procedure would be repeated twice more, the coffee each time amassing more and more foam at the top. After the grounds were allowed to settle, the host would pour the black, syrupy concoction into tiny egg-shaped porcelain cups, making sure each guest received some of the foam. The host would serve the most honored guest first, and it would be a grave insult for a guest not to accept and finish the drink.

If you don't wish to invest in a Turkish brass hand grinder (which is also an impressive tool for grinding black pepper) or in an ibrit, you can still make good Turkish coffee in a saucepan. Grind freshly roasted coffee as fine as you can and place one heaping teaspoon per person in the pan. Add one very small cup of cold water and one or two teaspoons of sugar per serving and mix it well. Bring this to a gentle boil and remove from heat. Repeat the procedure twice more and let the grounds settle for five minutes (adding a drop of cold water to aid this process, if you wish). Pour the coffee into small cups, making sure to give each person a bit of foam. Drink slowly, in small slurps. Contrary to American etiquette, in Turkey one is expected to drink noisily. This is a sign that you are enjoying your hot coffee, and it is not unusual for each person to swallow between five and ten small cups in one short sitting. But be forewarned: do not let anyone tell you that it is the custom to swallow the grounds. It never is, nor should it be, because they taste just awful, as I once unwittingly discovered. Instead, you might want to have the grounds read by someone who's an expert at that sort of thing. Like tea leaves, coffee grounds were often used as a medium for fortune-telling. If you are caffeine sensitive, after five strong cups, your fortune will most certainly be ''You will have trouble sleeping for the next week.'' Of course, you can always brew it decaffeinated.

Coffee Concentrate by Cold Extraction

The cold extraction method is not popular with most serious coffee drinkers because it is time-consuming and produces a rather flat tasting cup of coffee. However, it does produce a good coffee concentrate for use in cooking; this concentrate is over four times as strong as the regular brewed stuff, and it keeps for weeks in the refrigerator. It is useful in recipes that call for strong or double-strength coffee; it can be used with many of the recipes in this book.

To make coffee concentrate: steep one pound of medium-fine-ground coffee in 8 cups of cold water for twenty-four hours. Filter the mixture well and refrigerate the essence. When you want to make a cup of coffee add ¼ cup of concentrate to ¾ cup hot water. Stir and drink up. You will notice that the coffee lacks all aroma. This occurs because cold water cannot dissolve any of the aromatic oils as can hot water. On the flip side, however, those aromatic oils also contain acids, and the resulting cup is therefore easier on the stomach. If you love coffee but have problems with its acidity, try this method and see. It may be just the solution you've been waiting for.

Moka Pot for Espresso

You do not need to go to a café to enjoy a cup of rich espresso coffee, nor do you need to invest hundreds of dollars in a highly ornate brass espresso machine. The smartly designed pressurized Moka pot is an inexpensive alternative that makes a good cup of espresso anytime you want it. Made of heavy stainless steel (avoid aluminum pots, which can taint the brew with a metallic aftertaste), this pot has two chambers that screw together encapsulating a filter basket in the center, much like the flip-drip. The bottom pot is sealed off, and the pressure created there causes the water to boil at a higher than normal temperature. High-pressure steam is then forced up through the filter basket, past the coffee, and then into a thin tube running down the middle of the top chamber. The coffee-scented steam rushes through the tube and condenses into foamy black espresso coffee.

You will need to buy a Moka pot that is just the right size for your coffee-making needs, because you must make a full pot every time or your coffee will be weak and watery. Fill the bottom portion with cold water and place the filter basket inside it. Fill the filter to the top with finely ground, darkly roasted coffee and pack it down with a spoon. Screw on the top of the pot and place it over medium heat. When you hear the first gurgle of steam condensing to water, lower the heat and wait until the gurgling stops. Pour the rich drink from the top part of the pot and serve it black, in small cups with a twist of lemon peel, if you like it. You may sweeten the espresso, but do not add milk, which would dilute the creamy consistency of a well-made cup. The Moka pot produces a slightly more bitter espresso than the kind you order up in a cafe. This is because the steam overextracts the grounds, unlike the elaborate espresso machines used in cafés. However, a dash of sugar helps smooth things out.

Espresso Machine

In 1946 Achille Gaggia, an Italian, developed the first espresso machine to make a smooth cup. Before that, espresso was made by large amounts of steam pressure, which overextracted the grounds and made a bitter brew. In Italian, the word *espresso* means "fast," and that is how the coffee is brewed, allowing a fresh cup of coffee to be made for each patron. The very first espresso machine, shown at the 1855 Paris Exposition by Edward Santais, made two thousand cups in one hour. Although the crowds delighted in the concept, they found the drink too bitter, and had to wait almost one hundred years for Gaggia's steamless model.

Today anyone can own a small, countertop espresso machine. They are available with a lever for the energetic coffee lover to pump or with a small button to press, which automatically does the pumping for you. Either type will produce a superior cup to enjoy in the comfort of your own home.

PART TWO

✸ ✸ ✸

RECIPES

INGREDIENTS

Since you have taken the time and energy to select and purchase the very best coffee beans that you can find, when using them for cooking you will want to select the very best of all the other ingredients as well. Anything less would be an insult to your beautiful beans. Here are some tips for selecting and using the best.

Coffee Extract: Coffee extract is a simple way to impart coffee flavor to many dishes. Unlike instant coffee powder, which is hard to find, and instant coffee granules, which must be dissolved in water before being added to your dish, coffee extract can be added directly to the other ingredients without fuss. Coffee extract alone may not result in a deep enough coffee flavor, however, and sometimes I use it in addition to other coffee flavorings to intensify them.

Coffee extract is now becoming available in large grocery stores, and you can also order it by mail from Dean & Deluca, La Cuisine, and Maid of Scandinavia (see Sources at the end of this book). I order a few bottles at a time, as it keeps indefinitely and I seem to be constantly using a drop here or there.

Coffee Concentrate: A good substitute for coffee extract, coffee concentrate is made by steeping ground coffee beans in cold water for twenty-four hours. The recipe below will make two cups of concentrate, which will keep, well covered, in the refrigerator for up to two weeks, after which its flavor will start to deteriorate. Whenever a recipe calls for coffee extract, use the concentrate instead. You may need to use a bit more (1½ times the recommended amount) to achieve the same flavor, depending upon how strong your concentrate is. Taste your mixture frequently.

To make coffee extract: mix 2 cups of cold water with ¼ pound finely ground coffee beans in a jar or container with a tight-fitting lid. Cover the mixture and chill it for 24 hours. Strain it into a clean jar or container, cover, and refrigerate.

Instant Coffee: Instant coffee is available either powdered or in granules, and it is useful when your recipe cannot accommodate any additional liquid. Powder is easier to use because it does not have to be dissolved first in liquid, as granules do. But both can leave a bitter aftertaste, and so they must be used with discretion and in less delicate preparations.

Espresso Powder: Medaglia d'Oro, the most readily available instant espresso powder, is an excellent choice of flavoring. Unlike granules, it does not need to be dissolved before being used in a recipe. It is a very good product.

Coffee Beans: Coffee beans are used in a variety of forms in the upcoming recipes. They can be used to flavor a liquid by infusion, as with milk when making custard, or they can be ground and sprinkled directly into food as a spice. You will find many more uses for the beans as you learn to work with their unique characteristics.

Mocca Beans: These are not chocolate-covered coffee beans, but rather solid bittersweet chocolate fashioned to look like coffee beans. They make an attractive and suitable decoration for cakes and pastries containing coffee. They are available in many coffee specialty stores and by mail from Dean & Deluca, La Cuisine, and Maid of Scandinavia (see Sources).

Butter: Use only unsalted butter when it is called for in a recipe. This will be the case for most of the baked goods in this book, especially those whose flavor depends heavily upon the butter used. It is a good idea to use unsalted butter all the time because it is generally of a better quality than the salted stuff. However, if you need to use up the last of the salted butter in your refrigerator, use it for strong-flavored food like soups. Just be aware that the salt will cause the butter to burn faster than the unsalted kind. Mixing butter with a bit of oil will help raise its burning point. This trick applies to any type of butter.

If you would like to use margarine instead of butter for health reasons, go ahead; just keep in mind that the flavor will be different from that of the buttery version.

Oil: Olive oil is my choice for most of the sautéing I do. Use the best quality extra-virgin olive oil you can afford. Extra-virgin oil is derived from the first—or ''virgin''— pressing of the olive. Sometimes the label will also say ''cold-pressed'' oil. This signifies a purer, better quality oil. All extra-virgin oils are cold-pressed, but not all cold-pressed oils are extra-virgin, so read the label carefully. Colavita is a good, easily obtainable, and reasonably priced brand that I recommend for cooking. For salads and other raw uses, choose an even more flavorful one, preferably an oil imported from Italy, although France and California are now also producing excellent oils. I used to hold to the notion that the darker and murkier the oil was, the stronger the flavor was likely to be. I have since been proven wrong on occasion, but I still believe that is a useful test.

For flavorless oils, use anything without saturated fat. This is for reasons of health, not flavor. Corn oil will likely be cheaper than the highly touted canola oil, and it is just as healthful. There are also some flavorless olive oils, but they tend to be expensive and are not worth the higher price. Save your money to spend on the extra-virgin oil.

Flavored oils—oils imbued with various herbs and spices such as basil, garlic, and mustard seed—are a new trend on the market. I didn't use them in this book, but if you would like to try them in any of the recipes, please do. Substitution and variation will keep your cooking interesting and alive, and I always recommend it.

Eggs: All recipes in this book were tested with grade-A large eggs. Using medium or extra-large eggs will not ruin a recipe, but it may affect the texture and flavor, especially if many eggs are called for.

Make sure your eggs are fresh. With the threat of salmonella becoming more and more prevalent, this is very important in recipes calling for raw eggs, such as mousses and mayonnaise. To tell if an egg is fresh, carefully drop it into a pan of cold water. It should sink directly to the bottom, without bobbing around on top. If it floats, throw it out. Eggshells are porous, and the longer they sit around, the more air they will absorb. The captured air makes the egg more buoyant. Eggs kept in the carton will stay fresh longer than eggs placed in the little cup-shaped egg holders in your refrigerator because their shells are protected.

Many recipes in this book call for either egg whites or

egg yolks. You can freeze leftover whites and yolks in small containers (yogurt containers are practical) for several months. Defrost them slowly in the refrigerator before you use them.

Don't be intimidated by recipes that call for folding beaten egg whites into a batter. Although you must be careful not to deflate them, if you are patient and fold them slowly and gently *by hand,* this won't happen. Only people looking for shortcuts will be short-ended in their results.

Milk: When whole milk is specified, use it; otherwise feel free to use skim or low-fat. I use skim milk wherever possible to avoid the extra fat. However, that extra fat is frequently necessary in baked goods and rich foods, where it acts as a tenderizer, stabilizer, and preservative.

You may substitute regular milk with added lemon juice (1–2 tablespoons per quart) for buttermilk. Yogurt is a better substitute for buttermilk than milk and lemon juice because it has more of that familiar tang instead of just a sour edge.

When creme is specified, always use heavy creme. Many of the beverage recipes call for heavy cream, either whipped or plain. There is no acceptable substitute for real cream, so if your diet does not allow it, better to leave it out completely than to substitute. In baked goods, you can substitute milk for cream, but the texture may not be quite as moist.

Flour: All-purpose flour is used in most recipes in this book, with cake flour being called for only occasionally. When cake flour is specified, make sure to use plain cake flour, and not the self-rising kind. Unbleached is better than bleached for environmental reasons, but there is no difference in flavor. You can use stone-ground white flour for any of the recipes in the book, but do not use whole wheat flour, or the texture and flavor will be dramatically different.

Sugar: White sugar, brown sugar, and powdered (confectioner's) sugar are all used for different purposes in this book, and it is not a great idea to substitute one for another, as each of these sugars has a different flavor and texture that will impart a certain desired quality to the dish. Brown sugar can be either light or dark; just bear in mind that the dark variety has a more intense flavor. Use only light brown sugar in candy recipes; the dark brown sugar burns too easily during the necessary long cooking. You can substitute white sugar and a bit of molasses for brown sugar if you need to.

Honey, Molasses, and Maple Syrup: You can use an amber grade-C maple syrup (as opposed to the more expensive grade-A) for cooking without any adverse affects. When buying molasses, choose the unsulfured kind; Grandma's is a good, reliable, and easily available brand. If you would like to substitute honey for sugar in a recipe, you may do so, but make sure to decrease the liquid accordingly. Use a light honey rather than one whose flavor will overpower the dish. If your honey has crystallized, simply warm it up in the microwave or in a pan of hot water on the stove; it will return to its liquid state.

Chocolate: A perfect complement to coffee, chocolate is one of the most delicious and temperamental ingredients you will be working with. Most of the recipes in this book call for bittersweet chocolate because that is my personal favorite. Cooking with it also gives me an excuse to keep it around the house where I can nibble at it in the middle of the night. The quality of chocolate varies greatly. I find that imported European chocolate is consistently better than the American brands, although there are some exceptions, such as Ghirardelli and Nestlé Chocolat Côte d'Or. My favorite of all chocolates is Valrhona Extra Bitter, with Lindt Excellence and Callebaut as close seconds. Lindt has the added attraction of being available in many supermarkets across the country. They are all also available by mail from La Cuisine and Dean & Deluca.

Lindt also makes a milk chocolate called Mocca which is flavored with coffee. I like to use this occasionally, but on the whole I prefer to work with dark chocolate and coffee flavoring for a more intense flavor. White chocolate is also quite delicious with coffee, as its sweetness combines particularly well with coffee's bitterness.

Store bittersweet chocolate in an airtight wrapper in a cool, dry place, *not* in the refrigerator. It will keep almost indefinitely, if you have more willpower than I. White chocolate and milk chocolate have a shorter life span and will likely last no more than a year. Your chocolate may develop gray streaks, known as "bloom," but this will not affect the flavor—only the appearance, which will not matter if you are cooking with it.

When buying cocoa powder, choose a Dutch-processed brand. In the Dutch process, a bit of alkali is added to the cocoa; this makes it dissolve more easily and improves the flavor as well. Droste's is readily available in boxes in every large supermarket. Lindt also makes excellent cocoa, but it is hard to find.

Herbs and Spices: Use the very best, freshest herbs and the most intense-flavored spices you can find, for these two ingredients can make or break many a dish.

Most green leafy fresh herbs are pretty well interchangeable. Each herb will impart a different flavor to the dish, but if you choose an herb whose flavor you enjoy, this will be to your advantage. When a recipe calls for an herb you do not appreciate (as is frequently true of cilantro, whose strong flavor displeases some people), substitute one you like. I myself am not a tarragon fan, and frequently use thyme or rosemary instead. If you are fortunate enough to have a garden, or at least a sunny window, you can grow your own herbs. An herb window is particularly convenient in the winter when fresh herbs are expensive and scarce.

You can use dried herbs in place of fresh herbs, and vice versa. Use three times the amount of fresh herbs in place of dried, and similarly, use only one-third the amount of dried in place of fresh. In most cases, fresh herbs really make the difference between a good dish and a great one, so go out of your way to find them.

Spices add depth and character to a recipe, especially when they are fresh and full of flavor. The most frequently used spices are undeniably salt and pepper. Use freshly ground sea salt for the best flavor, and always, always use *freshly ground* whole peppercorns. This in itself will make a tremendous difference in your cooking.

Most spices have a shelf life of one to two years when stored in well-sealed containers in a cool, dry, dark place. After that they will have lost most of their flavor and should be thrown out. Buy spices in bulk at health food or ethnic stores if you can; they will probably be fresher, and undoubtedly be cheaper than the supermarket kind. I like to store them in small tins or glass jars, although they will be fine double-bagged in Ziploc bags. Don't forget to label them, or you won't be able to tell the mace from the coriander powder if you happen to have a stuffy nose.

Dried Fruits and Nuts: If you can buy your nuts in bulk, do so and you will save a good deal of money. If you buy an amount greater than what you are likely to use in the next three months, store the nuts in the freezer, tightly wrapped. The same rule applies to dried fruit.

Toasting the nuts before you use them greatly improves their flavor, making them more aromatic and intense. To toast nuts, spread them in a single layer on a baking sheet and bake them, stirring occasionally so they all brown evenly, for 15 to 20 minutes in a 375°F. oven. The nuts should be golden brown and your kitchen filled with their sweet scent. For slivered almonds or chopped nuts, the toasting time will be shorter because the smaller pieces will brown faster. Watch them carefully.

Dried fruit sometimes becomes too dry and hard to use. There are two ways to remedy this: you can soak the fruit in cold water, orange juice, rum, or some other liquid for an hour or until it is soft; or you can put the fruit in a sieve and pour boiling water over it. Some recipes direct you to soak dried fruit as a matter of course, especially when it is essential for the fruit to pick up the flavor of the soaking liquid.

Citrus Juice and Zest: Citrus zest is the colored part of the peel, without the bitter white pith underneath. You can use a specially made zester to scrape away the zest without catching any of the pith, but a vegetable peeler will work just as well. If you need to grate or grind the zest, you can chop it finely with a sharp knife or give it a spin in the food processor. You can also grate the zest directly off the fruit with a hand-held grater; however, I invariably end up with grated knuckles as well. It is easier, of course, to remove the zest before you cut into the fruit. I learned this the hard way.

If you are using a recipe that also calls for the juice of the fruit, halve the fruit and squeeze it over the zest. This will help keep the zest moist and flavorful. Citrus zest and juice will freeze well, so if you are in the mood, make a whole batch for later.

Beef and Chicken Stock: Homemade stock is best, of course, but the canned variety will do. Either buy a low-sodium brand or avoid adding salt to your recipe. Don't use bouillon cubes; they tend to be high in salt and low in flavor. Many also contain monosodium glutamate, which you or your guests may not be able to tolerate. A flavorful vegetable stock may be substituted in any recipe calling for meat stock.

BEVERAGES

CAFÉ AU LAIT

This is the quintessential breakfast drink in many parts of the world. It's called café con leche *in Spanish, and* caffellatte *in Italian. If you are sitting in a Paris café, you can also order this drink as a* café crème. *In any language this foamy mixture really satisfies first thing in the morning. Choose a dark roast, and serve this drink in big coffee bowls.*

1½ cups whole milk
1½ cups freshly brewed strong hot coffee

In a small saucepan bring the milk to a boil, whisking all the while to make it frothy. Or heat the milk to a boil, then whip it in a blender for 30 seconds. Or steam the milk in a pressurized steamer.

Simultaneously pour half the coffee and half the milk into each of two bowls. Spoon some of the froth on top. Serve immediately.

Serves 2

Note: One way to give your milk body, as suggested to me by my editor, Julia Banks, is to add a bit of honey to the milk, heat it in the microwave, then whisk the hot milk and honey for a few seconds and combine it with the coffee. This works particularly well if you like your coffee sweetened. The honey adds a delightful, subtle flavor and thickens the milk slightly. This method also works well with skim milk, whereas the traditional way will not.

CAFFÈ ALBERTO

This is my favorite way to drink coffee at my favorite café in New York City: Caffè Dante. Hot coffee is poured over vanilla, chocolate, or hazelnut gelati and served immediately. The trick is to quickly drink off the hot coffee before it melts the ice cream, creating a lukewarm puddle. Choose, a dark roast, and serve Caffè Alberto as a dessert.

**2 small scoops vanilla, chocolate, or hazelnut gelati
or ice cream
1½ cups freshly brewed strong hot coffee**

In each of two mugs, place a small scoop of gelati. Pour the hot coffee over the ice cream and serve at once.

Serves 2

CAFÉ MOKA VIENNOIS

The "moka" in the name of this drink stands for the chocolate; "viennois," for the whipped cream and cinnamon. If you wish to embellish this truly decadent combination, use a dark roast and add a jigger of cognac to each mug before topping with the whipped cream. Delicious!

  4 tablespoons grated bittersweet chocolate
1¾ cups freshly brewed strong hot coffee
**Whipped cream (either unsweetened or sweetened to
     taste)**
Ground cinnamon, for garnish
Extra grated bittersweet chocolate, for garnish
  2 jiggers cognac (optional)

Divide the grated chocolate between two mugs. Add the hot coffee and mix well. Add the cognac, if you wish.

Top each mug with whipped cream and sprinkle with cinnamon and grated chocolate. Serve immediately.

Serves 2

AROMATIC COFFEE I

The very first cups of coffee brewed by the Arabs sometimes contained fragrant spices and perfumes. This is a delightful updated version of the original.

Seeds from 4 green cardamom pods
¼ **teaspoon ground ginger**
¼ **teaspoon anise seeds**
 2 **whole black peppercorns**
 2 **whole cloves**
 5 **tablespoons dark-roasted coffee beans**
2–4 **teaspoons sugar, to taste (optional)**

Combine the cardamom seeds, ginger, anise seeds, peppercorns, cloves, and coffee beans in a coffee grinder and grind until fine.

Make espresso or Turkish coffee using the spiced coffee grounds.

Sweeten with sugar, if you wish, and serve immediately. Breathe deeply as you sip.

Serves 2

AROMATIC COFFEE II

In place of the traditional array of dry spices to scent and enhance espresso coffee, in this coffee I have used liquid flavorings to perfume a lighter brew. Drinking this cup is a very different experience, and I advise that you try them both.

 2 **cups freshly brewed strong hot coffee, in the pot**
 1 **teaspoon orange flower water**
¼ **teaspoon vanilla extract**
1–2 **teaspoons sugar, to taste (optional)**

To the coffee pot add the orange flower water, vanilla extract, and sugar, if you wish. Stir until the sugar is dissolved and the ingredients are combined.

Pour the scented coffee into two cups and serve immediately.

Serves 2

ICED COFFEE

Iced coffee is not necessarily a simple brew. You can use leftover breakfast coffee, cooled and iced, but don't even think about using yesterday's coffee. All the aroma will have disappeared, and you will be left with a flat, lifeless brew.

The most superior iced coffee is made with freshly brewed coffee and coffee ice cubes. To make coffee ice cubes, fill an ice cube tray with leftover coffee and freeze.

If you prefer a sweetened drink, add sugar to the hot coffee, or add some Coffee Syrup (see page 189) to chilled beverage.

Grated citrus rind and sliced oranges are refreshing additions, as are spices like cinnamon and cardamom. For a long drink, spike the coffee with vodka, Kahlúa, or Grand Marnier. Decisions, decisions!

1 quart freshly brewed strong coffee
Sugar to taste
Coffee or regular ice cubes
Milk or cream (optional)

Sweeten the hot coffee to taste with the sugar, place it in a container with a tight-fitting lid, and cover it well to preserve the aroma.

Let the coffee come to room temperature and then refrigerate until it is cold.

Fill tall glasses with ice cubes and pour in the cold coffee. Milk is a nice accompaniment, and cream even nicer.

Serves 4

COFFEE EGG CREAM

No, there is no egg in an egg cream, nor was there ever any. The name comes from the white froth that gathers at the top of the glass, resembling a beaten egg white. Egg creams, probably a New York City soda fountain creation, are composed of flavored syrup (Fox's or U-Bet brand chocolate syrup is traditional), seltzer, and milk.

If you have never had an egg cream, you are in for a delightful experience. If you have had one, please feel free to adjust the ingredients to suit your taste. Egg creams are a very personal undertaking.

1–2 tablespoons Coffee Syrup (see page 189), to taste
¾ cup ice-cold milk
⅓ cup ice-cold seltzer

In a tall soda glass, stir together the coffee syrup and the milk until they are well combined and uniform in color.

Slowly pour in the seltzer and watch the white bubbles foam above the rim of the glass. Stir very lightly to combine.

Sip slowly with a straw and think about the good old days, because egg creams are pure nostalgia.

Serves 1

Variations: To make a mocha egg cream, use half chocolate syrup and half coffee syrup, a particularly delicious twist. Another good idea is to make the coffee egg cream with a dash of vanilla extract or use half vanilla syrup. Of course, if you bring liqueurs into play, the nontraditional possibilities are endless.

HOT ALMOND COFFEE SUPREME

This luscious concoction falls somewhere between a beverage and a food. It makes a perfect coffee break treat that really satisfies those midafternoon hunger pangs. Or serve it for dessert when something light but sweet is required.

Sweet ground chocolate is a wonderful garnish for all kinds of drinks and desserts. It is available in specialty gourmet shops and by mail from Williams-Sonoma and Dean & Deluca (see page 255 for source listing).

 3 tablespoons finely chopped blanched almonds
 2 teaspoons butter
 2 cups freshly brewed strong hot coffee, in the pot
⅛ teaspoon almond extract
1–3 teaspoon sugar, or to taste
Whipped cream, for garnish (optional)
Sweet ground chocolate, for garnish (optional)

In a frying pan over medium-high heat sauté the almonds in the butter, stirring frequently, until they begin to brown and release their aroma.

To the coffee pot add the almond extract and the sugar and stir to dissolve. Taste and add more sugar if you wish.

Divide the coffee mixture between two cups, top with the whipped cream, if you wish, and sprinkle half the sautéed almonds on top. Dust the whole with the sweet ground chocolate and serve immediately with spoons. The hotter the coffee, the better.

Serves 2

BLACK-AND-WHITE CHOCOLATE COFFEE

I was introduced to a variant of this drink in the home of a chocolate-loving friend. The drink Eloise served me was hot cocoa laced with white chocolate, but I think this less sweet, coffee-flavored version is a nice variation.

Do use the cocoa for garnish even if you decide to skip the whipped cream; the bitterness is a nice foil against the sweet chocolate, which never quite melts into the hot coffee.

½ **cup whole milk or half-and-half**
 2 **tablespoons grated white chocolate**
 2 **tablespoons grated dark chocolate**
 2 **cups freshly brewed strong hot coffee**
Whipped cream for garnish (optional)
Cocoa powder for garnish (optional)

In a small saucepan over low heat, gently scald the milk or half-and-half. Remove from heat, cover to keep warm, and set aside.

In the bottom of each of two mugs place 1 tablespoon of grated white chocolate and 1 tablespoon of grated dark chocolate. Divide the coffee between the mugs and stir briefly. Slowly pour half of the warm milk into each mug. Garnish with the whipped cream and sprinkle a bit of cocoa powder on top. Serve immediately.

Serves 2

Variations: Add a jigger of Grand Marnier or Sabra, a chocolate-orange flavored liqueur, to each mug before topping with the whipped cream.

Add a dash of crème de menthe to the mixture. The subtle mint flavor does nice things to the coffee.

COFFEE PUNCH

This is the perfect drink to serve at a party. It has only a moderate amount of alcohol, and the coffee will help keep your guests lively well into the evening. If you would prefer a nonalcoholic drink, leave out the rum and liqueur.

Freeze coffee beans inside ice cubes, or use coffee ice cubes and float whole beans atop the punch.

You can double or triple the recipe for bigger parties.

 1 quart freshly brewed strong hot coffee
 1 liter ginger ale
 2 cups pineapple juice
 1 cup pear nectar
 1 pint rum
 ¼ cup Kahlúa or Tia Maria (optional)
 1 orange, thinly sliced
 1 lemon, thinly sliced
 1 lime, thinly sliced
Coffee ice cubes or coffee beans frozen inside ice
       cubes (optional)
Nutmeg

In a large punch bowl mix together the coffee, ginger ale, pineapple juice, pear nectar, rum, Kahlúa or Tia Maria, and the orange, lemon, and lime slices.

Add the ice cubes and any garnish you choose and stir well. Grate the nutmeg on the surface of the punch. Serve immediately.

Serves 12–15

CAFÉ MEJICANO

Kahlúa and spices add zip to each sip. Try serving this with coffee-flavored flan for dessert after a Mexican or Spanish meal. Use a dark-roast coffee.

 4 whole cloves
 2 jiggers Kahlúa
 2 cups freshly brewed strong hot coffee
 2 cinnamon sticks

In each of two mugs place 2 cloves and 1 jigger of Kahlúa. Stir in the hot coffee. Garnish with cinnamon sticks and serve immediately.

Serves 2

CAFFÈ SAMBUCA

A classic combination of licorice-flavored Sambuca liqueur and espresso coffee. Rub the lemon peel around the lip of the demitasse, if you like a citrus flavor in your coffee.

¾ **cup freshly brewed hot espresso**
2 **tablespoons Sambuca**
2 **slivers lemon peel (optional)**

Divide the espresso between two demitasses. Top each with half the Sambuca. Serve with lemon zest, if you wish.

Serves 2

CAFÉ BRÛLOT

Café Brûlot, a flaming concoction from New Orleans, is a dramatic way to end a meal. You can make the spicy sugar-citrus mixture in advance and ignite it at the last minute. Serve in tiny cups. Substitute Grand Marnier for the curaçao for an interesting variation. Use a dark-roast coffee for this beverage.

1-inch piece of cinnamon stick
5 cloves
Dash of freshly grated nutmeg
Finely grated zest of ½ lemon
Finely grated zest of ½ small orange
2–4 teaspoons sugar
⅓ cup brandy
 2 tablespoons curaçao
 3 cups freshly brewed strong hot coffee

Place the cinnamon, cloves, nutmeg, lemon zest, orange zest, and sugar in a mortar or a small bowl. With the pestle or with the back of a wooden spoon, bruise and mix the ingredients to release and integrate their flavors. Set the mixture aside; the longer it sits, the more fragrant your brew will be.

Just before serving, scald 6 demitasses with boiling water and cover them with a dish towel to keep warm.

Place the spice mixture in a chafing dish or small saucepan over a low flame. Add the brandy and the curaçao and gently heat the mixture, swirling, until the sugar begins to dissolve.

Bring the saucepan to the table side, if desired, and ignite the mixture. Let the flames die down and stir. Gradually add the hot coffee to the saucepan, stir to combine, and serve immediately in the warmed demitasses.

Serves 6

IRISH COFFEE

You don't need Celtic blood in your veins to enjoy this famous beverage. It will warm you all the same on chilly, rainy afternoons.

  3 ounces Irish whiskey
  2 teaspoons sugar
1¾ cups freshly brewed strong hot coffee
  3 tablespoons heavy cream

Divide the whiskey and the sugar between two glasses or mugs and stir until the sugar is dissolved. Add half of the hot coffee to each mug and stir. Taste and add more sugar if you wish.

Very slowly pour half of the cream over an inverted tablespoon so the cream drips onto the surface of the coffee and floats there. (Another way to do this is to gently pour a thin stream of cream down the side of the mug, but you will need big mugs for this to work.)

Serve immediately, and sip without mixing the cream into the coffee.

Serves 2

Variations: Whip the cream before floating it on top of the coffee.

Use scotch whisky for Scottish coffee.

CLASSIC CAPPUCCINO

Cappuccino, the heavenly elixir of espresso coffee and foam, is traditionally capped with a sprinkling of bitter cocoa powder. In this version, I use sweet ground chocolate (available from Williams-Sonoma and Dean & DeLuca, see Sources) because I think the coffee is bitter enough. If you prefer a bitter taste, substitute unsweetened cocoa.

⅔ **cup milk**
 1 **cup freshly brewed hot espresso**
Sweet ground chocolate for garnish

Steam the milk until it is thick and frothy, or slowly heat it in a small saucepan over low heat, beating with a whisk until it is hot and foamy. Or scald the milk on the stove or in a microwave, and then whip it in the blender for a few seconds.

Divide the espresso between two mugs. Carefully pour some of the hot milk into each mug. Gently top each mug with a bit of the foam. Be careful not to deflate it by stirring. Sprinkle a bit of sweet ground chocolate over the cappuccino. Serve immediately.

Serves 2

CINNAMON CAPPUCCINO

In this toasty version of cappuccino, a dash of cinnamon mingles with the grounds as the coffee brews, for a further nuance of the spice.

½ teaspoon ground cinnamon
6 tablespoons ground espresso beans
¾ cup milk
Ground cinnamon for garnish
2 cinnamon sticks for garnish (optional)

Mix the cinnamon with the ground espresso beans and brew the espresso as usual.

Steam the milk until it is thick and frothy, or heat it in a small saucepan over low heat, beating with a wire whisk until it is hot and foamy. Or scald the milk on the stove or in a microwave, and then whip it in the blender for a few seconds until it is fluffy.

Divide the cinnamon-scented espresso between two mugs. Carefully pour some of the hot milk into each mug, and gently top each mug with a bit of the foam, taking care not to deflate it by stirring.

Sprinkle ground cinnamon over the cappuccino. Garnish with a cinnamon stick, if you wish, and serve immediately.

Serves 2

CAFFÈ MACCHIATO

Caffè macchiato is similar to café au lait, except that less coffee is used in proportion to the milk. The result is a coffee-flavored hot milk beverage that is just the thing on mornings when you want to enjoy a steaming cup of coffee without becoming too alert.

1⅓ cups milk
½ cup freshly brewed hot coffee

Steam the milk until it is thick and frothy, or slowly heat it in a saucepan over low heat, beating with a whisk until it is hot and foamy. Or scald the milk on the stove or in a microwave, and then whip it in the blender for a few seconds until it is fluffy.

Into each of two mugs, simultaneously pour half of the milk and half of the coffee. Serve immediately.

Serves 2

DOUBLE CHOCOLATE MOCHACCINO

This is probably the most chocolaty mochaccino you will ever indulge in! By imbuing both the milk and the coffee with chocolate, you can create the mocha lover's daily-double. Sweet ground chocolate is available by mail from Williams-Sonoma and Dean & Deluca (see Sources*).*

 4 tablespoons sweet ground chocolate
¾ cup milk
 1 cup freshly brewed hot espresso
Additional sweet ground chocolate for garnish

In a small bowl or saucepan whisk 2 tablespoons of the sweet ground chocolate into the milk, beating well to combine. Make sure there are no remaining lumps.

Steam the chocolate milk until it is thick and frothy, or slowly heat it in a small saucepan over low heat, beating with a whisk until the milk is hot and foamy. Or scald the milk on the stove or in a microwave, and then whip it in the blender for a few seconds until it is fluffy. Set aside. Divide the remaining 2 tablespoons of sweet ground chocolate between two mugs. Mix half the espresso into each and stir well to be sure the hot espresso has dissolved any lumps.

Carefully pour some of the chocolate milk into each espresso-filled mug. With a spoon, gently top each mug with a bit of the foam, taking care not to deflate it by stirring. Garnish each mug with a sprinkling of sweet ground chocolate. Serve immediately to chocolate loving friends.

Serves 2

CREAM-OF-THE-CROP COFFEE

Fattening? Yes. Worth it? Definitely. Serve this rich treat with, or in place of, dessert. Or serve it as an indulgent winter afternoon coffee break. It's just perfect on one of those Sundays where staying in bed all day is the only option.

½ **cup heavy cream**
2 **teaspoons sugar**
1¼ **cups freshly brewed hot coffee**
¼ **cup Baileys Irish Cream liqueur**
Dash of nutmeg

Whip the heavy cream with the sugar until the cream holds soft peaks. Set aside.

Divide the coffee between two mugs. Stir half of the Baileys Irish Cream liqueur into each mug. Top the mugs with a good-sized dollop of whipped cream and garnish with nutmeg. Serve immediately.

Serves 2

COFFEE TROPICANA

Orange zest, pineapple juice, and coconut-flavored rum enhance milky coffee for the sunniest cup of java you will ever drink.

1⅓ cups freshly brewed hot coffee
 ¼ cup milk
 1 tablespoon pineapple juice
 3 tablespoons coconut-flavored rum
 1 teaspoon grated orange zest

In a glass measuring cup mix the coffee, milk, and pineapple juice. Stir well.

Divide the coffee mixture between two mugs. Stir half the coconut-flavored rum into each mug. Garnish the mugs with the grated orange zest and serve immediately.

Serves 2

CAFFÈ AMARETTO

Sugary, hard amaretto cookies are often served with coffee in Italian cafés, but less often is the similarly flavored liqueur used directly in the brew. It's a shame, because the combination is sensational.

1½ cups freshly brewed hot coffee
¼ cup amaretto liqueur

Divide the coffee between two mugs. Top each mug with half of the amaretto liqueur. Serve black.

Serves 2

FRUIT BOWL COFFEE

This lively mixture of coffee and fruit liqueurs is especially apropos during the holiday season when something different and festive is called for.

2 tablespoons Chambord liqueur (raspberry-flavored liqueur)
2 tablespoons crème de cassis
2 tablespoons Calvados or applejack
1½ cups freshly brewed hot coffee
Cream or milk (optional)

In a glass measuring cup with a lip combine the Chambord liqueur, crème de cassis, and Calvados. Stir well and divide between two mugs.

Top each mug with half of the brewed coffee and stir well. Lighten with a bit of cream or milk, if desired.

Serves 2

VIETNAMESE COFFEE

This is my favorite dessert after a spicy Vietnamese meal. My favorite Vietnamese restaurant in New York City's Chinatown serves this drink in tall glasses. Sweetened condensed milk is mounded in the bottom of the glass, and piping hot espresso is poured over it. The two liquids stay separate until you mix them, and then the sugary milk tames the bitter coffee. This concoction is best served only to the sweet-toothed, but they will love it.

This coffee is also a treat when served iced.

¼ cup sweetened condensed milk
1 cup freshly brewed hot espresso

Spoon half of the condensed milk into each of two glasses. Gently pour half the espresso over the milk in each glass; the espresso will rest on top of the milk.

Either stir the coffee and milk together or drink it as is, but do serve it immediately before the espresso cools.

Serves 2

COCONUT COFFEE

I first had this coffee in a small Afghan restaurant on St. Marks Place in Manhattan. It is a mildly sweet finale to any meal, but is especially pleasant after a spicy one.

This coffee is also nice iced; just make sure to mix in the coconut milk while the coffee is still hot so it dissolves evenly. Then let the whole batch cool and serve it in tall glasses with ice cubes and long straws.

1½ **cups freshly brewed hot coffee**
 ⅓ **cup cream of coconut**
 2 **teaspoons sweetened flaked coconut**

Divide the hot coffee between two mugs. Top each mug with half of the coconut cream and stir well to combine.

Float one teaspoon of coconut flakes on top of each mug. Serve immediately.

Serves 2

COOKIES

RUSSIAN COFFEE COOKIES

Because rye flourishes in the colder climate of northern Russia, it is not unusual to find it in cookies and pastries as well as in bread. These cookies are not overly sweet, but they are fragrant and nutty from the rye flour.

¾ **cup rye flour**
¾ **cup all-purpose flour**
½ **cup sugar**
¼ **teaspoon salt**
½ **cup butter (1 stick), cut into pieces**
 2 **tablespoons molasses**
¼ **cup double-strength cold brewed coffee**

In a food processor, combine the flours, sugar, and salt and pulse to mix. Add the butter and pulse until the mixture resembles cornmeal. Gently mix in the molasses and coffee and pulse until the mixture forms a ball. Wrap well and refrigerate for at least three hours and up to three days. (The dough may also be frozen for two months and defrosted before proceeding.)

Heat the oven to 350°F. and lightly grease several baking sheets.

On a very lightly floured work surface, roll the dough ⅛ inch thick and cut with a 2-inch round cookie cutter. Place cookies 1 inch apart on prepared baking sheets and prick them decoratively with the tines of a fork. Bake for about 10 minutes, until they are pale gold around the edges.

Transfer the cookies to a rack to cool. Store them in airtight containers at room temperature for up to two weeks.

Makes about 60 cookies

MOCHA CHIP COOKIES

These cookies are close relatives of regular chocolate chip cookies, with extra chocolate and coffee as an added inducement to finish the whole batch warm from the oven.

1¼ cups (2½ sticks) butter at room temperature
  1 cup confectioner's sugar
  ½ cup brown sugar
  ¼ teaspoon salt
  2 tablespoons instant coffee powder
  1 tablespoon hot water
  ½ teaspoon coffee extract
2½ cups all-purpose flour
  2 teaspoons baking powder
  2 cups chocolate chips
  ½ cup granulated sugar for rolling the cookies in

Heat the oven to 350°F. and lightly grease several baking sheets.

Cream the butter, confectioner's sugar, brown sugar, and salt with an electric mixer until very creamy, about 2 minutes. Dissolve the instant coffee in the hot water, and stir into the butter mixture. Add the coffee extract and beat well.

Sift together the flour and baking powder, and gradually add the dry ingredients to the batter, stirring just until incorporated. Fold in the chocolate chips.

Shape dough into 1-inch balls, roll in the granulated sugar, and place 1 inch apart on prepared baking sheets. Bake for about 15 minutes, until they are a pale golden brown.

Transfer cookies to a rack to cool. Store them in airtight containers at room temperature for up to two weeks.

Makes about 60 cookies

COCONUT-COFFEE COOKIES

My favorite Afghan restaurant in New York serves coffee sweetened with coconut milk, and this terrific duo also works particularly well in a chewy cookie. Coconut milk is available in Asian markets and some large supermarkets. Do not use cream of coconut, which is much sweeter and thicker and will result in a gloppy mess.

½ **cup (1 stick) butter at room temperature**
¾ **cup sugar**

¼ **teaspoon salt**
1 **egg**
½ **cup coconut milk**
2 **tablespoons instant coffee powder**
1½ **cups all-purpose flour**
1 **teaspoon baking powder**
1 **cup flaked coconut**

Heat the oven to 350°F. and lightly grease several baking sheets.

Cream the butter, sugar, and salt with an electric mixer until creamy, about 1 minute. Add the egg and beat well. Heat the coconut milk in a small saucepan over medium heat or in the microwave. Add the instant coffee and stir to dissolve it. Stir this into the butter mixture.

Sift together the flour and baking powder, and gradually add to the batter, stirring just until the dry ingredients are incorporated. Fold in the coconut flakes.

Drop rounded teaspoons of the batter 1 inch apart on prepared baking sheets. Bake the cookies for 12 to 15 minutes, until they are a pale golden brown.

Transfer the cookies to a rack to cool. Store them in airtight containers at room temperature for up to two weeks.

Makes about 45 cookies

COFFEE RUM COOKIES

Coffee and rum are a terrific combination in hot drinks and in these cookies. Although the nuts are optional, they add a pleasant crunch.

¾ cup (1½ sticks) butter at room temperature
1 cup sugar
½ teaspoon salt
⅓ cup dark rum
2 tablespoons instant coffee powder
3 cups all-purpose flour
2 teaspoons baking powder
1 cup toasted hazelnuts (optional)
Confectioner's sugar for dusting

Heat the oven to 375°F. and lightly grease several baking sheets.

Cream the butter, sugar, and salt with an electric mixer until it is light and fluffy, about 1 minute. Heat the rum in a small saucepan over low heat or in the microwave. Add the instant coffee and stir to dissolve. Add to butter mixture and beat well.

Sift together the flour and baking powder, and gradually add the dry ingredients to the batter, stirring until just incorporated. Fold in the nuts, if you are using them.

Shape the dough into 1-inch balls and place them 1½ inches apart on the prepared baking sheets. Flatten each cookie with the tines of a fork, making a crisscross pattern on the top. Bake for 12 to 15 minutes until the edges just begin to brown.

Transfer the cookies to a rack to cool, and dust them with the confectioner's sugar. Store them in airtight containers at room temperature for up to two weeks.

Makes about 45 cookies

KAHLÚA-PECAN BARS

These decadent bars are best cut very small, or their richness can become cloying. Served in tiny portions, however, these lush, chewy beauties are always a tremendous success.

For the Crust:
 ½ cup (1 stick) butter
 1 cup brown sugar
 1½ cups all-purpose flour
 ½ cup toasted pecans
 1 teaspoon vanilla extract
 ⅛ teaspoon salt

Heat oven to 350°F. Line a 9 × 13-inch baking pan with wax paper and grease lightly.

Place all of the ingredients in a food processor and pulse until they are combined but still crumbly.

Evenly press the crust mixture into the prepared baking pan. Bake until pale golden brown around the edges, 15 to 20 minutes.

For the Filling:
 2 eggs
 ¼ teaspoon salt
 ½ cup granulated sugar
 ½ cup brown sugar
 ¼ cup cold brewed coffee
 ¼ cup Kahlúa
 ⅓ cup flour
 1 teaspoon baking powder
 1 cup coarsely chopped toasted pecans
Confectioner's sugar for dusting (optional)

Beat the eggs, salt, and sugars with an electric mixer until thick and creamy, about 3 minutes. Blend in the coffee and Kahlúa. Sift together the flour and baking powder, and beat the dry ingredients into the egg mixture until the batter looks thick and pale, about 5 minutes. Fold in the pecans.

Pour the filling onto the crust, and bake for 25 minutes, or until the top is set and golden brown. Cool completely before cutting into bars. Store in an airtight container in the refrigerator for up to four days. Dust the cookies with confectioner's sugar before serving, if you wish.

Makes about 60 bars

ESPRESSO-ANISE WAFERS

Inspired by the succulent Italian combination of espresso and Sambuca, I made these cookies to re-create that balance of flavors in a portable form.

2 cups (4 sticks) butter at room temperature
1 cup sugar
½ teaspoon salt
1 egg
½ cup cold brewed espresso
2 tablespoons Sambuca
4 cups all-purpose flour
1 teaspoon baking powder
1 teaspoon cinnamon
2 teaspoons crushed anise seeds
1 lightly beaten egg white

Cream the butter, sugar, and salt with an electric mixer until creamy, about 1 minute. Add the egg and beat well. Mix in the espresso and Sambuca a few tablespoons at a time, and beat until well combined.

Sift together the flour, baking powder, cinnamon, and anise seeds, and gently add the dry ingredients to the butter mixture, stirring until just combined. Shape the dough into a ball, wrap it well, and refrigerate it for at least three hours, and up to three days. The dough may also be frozen for two months and defrosted before proceeding.

Heat the oven to 350°F. and lightly grease several baking sheets.

On a very lightly floured surface, roll the dough ¼ inch thick and cut it with a 2-inch decorative cookie cutter. Place the cookies 1 inch apart on the prepared baking sheets and brush them with the beaten egg white. Bake the cookies for 12 to 15 minutes, until they are pale golden around the edges.

Transfer the cookies to a rack to cool. Store them in airtight containers at room temperature for up to two weeks.

Makes about 60 cookies

COFFEE-GINGER THINS

These are delicate, buttery, highly sophisticated cookies that go as nicely with a glass of dessert wine as they do with an espresso.

½ cup (1 stick) butter at room temperature
⅔ cup sugar
2 tablespoons instant coffee powder
1 tablespoon hot water or hot coffee
⅓ cup mild honey
1 teaspoon ground ginger
1 cup all-purpose flour
¼ teaspoon salt
½ finely chopped crystallized ginger

Heat the oven to 325°F. and grease several cookie sheets.

Cream the butter and sugar with an electric mixer until it is fluffy and light, about 1 minute. Dissolve the coffee in the water and it add to the butter mixture. Stir in the honey and the ground ginger. Gradually add the flour and the salt, stirring only until the mixture is combined. Fold in the crystallized ginger.

Drop teaspoons of batter onto the prepared cookie sheets at least two inches apart. Bake the cookies for 12 to 14 minutes, watching carefully so they don't burn. When they look lightly browned and lacy, they are ready.

Cool the cookies on the baking sheets for a few minutes, and then transfer them with a spatula to a rack to finish cooling. Store them in airtight containers at room temperature for up to five days.

Makes about 40 cookies

COFFEE PECAN STICKS

These cookies are a breeze to make. You can store the dough in the freezer, then slice and bake the cookies whenever you need a quick cookie fix.

¾ cup (1½ sticks) butter at room temperature
½ teaspoon salt
¾ cup firmly packed light brown sugar
 1 egg
 2 teaspoons coffee extract
 2 cups all-purpose flour
 1 teaspoon baking soda
¼ cup toasted pecans, finely chopped

Cream the butter, salt, and brown sugar with an electric mixer until light and creamy, about 1 minute. Add the egg and coffee extract and beat well.

Sift together the flour and baking soda, and gradually add the dry ingredients to the butter mixture, stirring lightly until they are just incorporated. Do not overmix or the crumb will toughen. Fold in the pecans.

Place the dough on a long strip of wax paper or plastic wrap, and shape it into a long, thin log. (You can divide the dough in half and make two short, thin rolls if you find them easier to work with.) Wrap the dough well and refrigerate it for at least two hours, and up to three days. The dough may be frozen at this point.

Heat the oven to 350°F. and lightly grease two baking sheets.

Unwrap the dough and cut it into ¼-inch slices. (If it is frozen, allow it to soften slightly, but it is not necessary to defrost it.) Place the cookies about ½ inch apart on the prepared baking sheets, and chill for ten minutes. (This will help the cookies retain their shape.) Bake until golden brown, 10 to 12 minutes.

With a spatula, transfer the cookies to a wire rack to cool. Store them in airtight containers at room temperature for up to two weeks.

Makes about 40 cookies

ESPRESSO SHORTBREAD

Finely ground espresso powder is the principle flavoring in this recipe, which makes an aromatic cookie with a pleasant, slightly bitter undertone. Use a light Viennese-style roast; anything darker would overpower the delicate butter flavor that makes shortbread so special. Although you could embellish these simple cookies by adding nuts or chocolate, or by rolling them in special sugar before baking, I think they are best when served plain—classic and elegant.

  1 cup (2 sticks) butter at room temperature
  ½ teaspoon salt
  ¾ cup sugar
2⅓ cups cake flour
  1 tablespoon finely ground espresso beans

With an electric mixer, cream the butter, salt, and sugar until the mixture is light and creamy, about 1 minute. Gradually add the flour and ground espresso beans, mixing lightly until just incorporated. Do not overmix or the crumb will toughen.

Place the dough on a long strip of wax paper or plastic wrap, and shape it into a long, thin log. (You can divide the dough in half and make two short, thin rolls if you find them easier to work with.) Wrap the dough well and refrigerate it for at least four hours, and up to three days. The dough may be frozen at this point.

Heat the oven to 300°F., and line two baking sheets with parchment or wax paper.

Unwrap the dough and cut it into ¼-inch slices. (If it is frozen, allow it to soften slightly, but it is not necessary to defrost it.) Place the cookies about ½ inch apart on the prepared baking sheets, and bake until firm, 12 to 15 minutes. Do not allow the cookies to brown.

With a spatula, transfer the cookies to a wire rack to cool. Store them in airtight containers at room temperature for up to two weeks.

Makes about 60 cookies

SESAME DUNKING WAFERS

These plain buttery cookies are utterly delicious! You must try them even if you think you are indifferent to sesame. Dunk them in strong, thick espresso for a very special treat.

¾ cup sesame seeds
½ cup (1 stick) butter at room temperature
1 teaspoon vanilla extract
¼ teaspoon salt
1 cup sugar
1 egg
2 cups all-purpose flour
¼ cup milk

Toast the sesame seeds in a large frying pan over medium heat, stirring constantly, until they turn golden brown and release their scent. Watch carefully as these can go from golden brown to bitter black in seconds.

Cream the butter with the vanilla, salt, and sugar with an electric mixer until light and creamy, about 1 minute. Beat in the egg. Gradually add half of the flour, then all of the milk, followed by the rest of the flour. Mix lightly until the ingredients are just incorporated. Do not overmix or the crumb will toughen. Fold in the sesame seeds.

Place the dough on a long strip of wax paper or plastic wrap, and shape it into a long, thin log. (You can divide the dough in half and make two short, thin rolls if you find them easier to work with.) Wrap the dough well and freeze it overnight or up to three months.

Heat the oven to 375°F.

Unwrap the dough and cut it into ¼-inch slices. Place them about 1 inch apart on lightly greased sheets, and bake until the edges turn gold brown, about 15 minutes.

With a spatula, transfer the cookies to a wire rack to cool. Store them in airtight containers at room temperature for up to two weeks.

Makes about 50 cookies

BUTTERSCOTCH COFFEE SQUARES

These are a close cousin to chewy blondies but with a definite coffee flavor. Although I love them most just eaten out of hand, if you want to jazz these squares up a bit, you might warm them and serve them with ice cream. Everybody will like these.

¾ **cup (1½ sticks) butter**
 2 **cups firmly packed dark brown sugar**

2 tablespoons instant coffee powder
2 eggs
1 tablespoon vanilla extract
2 cups all-purpose flour
½ teaspoon salt
2 teaspoons baking powder
1 cup chopped walnuts
1 cup chocolate chips (optional)

Heat the oven to 350°F. and grease a 9 × 13-inch baking pan.

Melt the butter and the brown sugar in a large saucepan over a low flame. Stir constantly until the mixture is well combined, and add the coffee powder, stirring to dissolve it. When the mixture feels barely warm to the touch, beat in the eggs and vanilla until smooth.

Sift the flour, salt, and baking powder together, and stir the dry ingredients into the coffee mixture. Fold in the nuts and add the chocolate chips, if you wish.

Pour the batter into the prepared pan, smooth out the top with a spatula, and bake for 25 minutes or until lightly browned. These cookies are ready even before a tester inserted in the center comes out clean, and in order to maintain their chewiness it is important not to overbake them. Watch them carefully.

Cool the cookies on a rack, and then cut them into squares. Store them in airtight containers in the refrigerator for up to four days.

Makes 24 squares

COFFEE NUT KISSES

Since there is no flour in these airy puffs, they are an ideal Passover dessert. My friend Susan is always looking for new Passover recipes, and I made these with her in mind. You may use any type of nut you wish instead of the almonds.

1¾ cups toasted almonds
¼ cup whole coffee beans
1½ cups sugar
  2 egg whites
  1 teaspoon vanilla extract
Mocca beans (optional)

Heat the oven to 325°F. Lightly grease two baking sheets.

In a food processor or a blender, finely grind the almonds and coffee beans with half of the sugar. Add the egg whites and process until well combined. Scrape the sides of the container with a rubber spatula. Add the rest of the sugar and the vanilla extract and blend well.

Shape the dough into 1-inch balls, and place them about ½ inch apart on the prepared baking sheets. Top with mocca beans, if desired. Bake until firm and lightly colored, about 20 minutes.

With a spatula, transfer the cookies to a wire rack to cool. Store them in airtight containers at room temperature for up to one week.

Makes about 40 cookies

MOCHA-FILLED SABLÉS

These beautiful cookies make a delightful gift for the sweet-toothed. If you do not have scallop-shaped cookie cutter, you can substitute any other pattern measuring about 2 inches in diameter.

1¾ cups all-purpose flour
½ cup sugar
4 hard-boiled egg yolks, mashed
¼ teaspoon salt
½ teaspoon vanilla extract
¾ cup (1½ sticks) butter, cut into pieces
8 ounces bittersweet chocolate, chopped
1 tablespoon instant espresso powder
2 teaspoons hot water

Combine the flour, sugar, egg yolks, salt, vanilla extract and butter in a food processor and pulse to combine. Shape the dough into a ball, wrap it in plastic, and refrigerate it for 20 minutes.

Heat the oven to 375°F. and lightly grease two baking sheets.

On a lightly floured work surface, roll the dough ⅛ inch thick. Use a scallop-shaped cookie cutter to cut the dough, and place the cookies 1 inch apart on the prepared baking sheets. Gather the scraps and re-roll until all the dough is used. If the dough becomes too soft to work with, refrigerate it for a few minutes before proceeding. When all of the cookies are cut, refrigerate the baking sheets for fifteen minutes so the cookies will keep their shape while baking.

Bake the cookies for 10 to 12 minutes, until the edges are barely golden. Transfer them to a wire rack to cool.

Melt the chocolate in the top of a double boiler over simmering water, stirring constantly. Dissolve the espresso powder in the hot water, and mix it with the chocolate. Allow the mixture to cool until it is thick enough to spread.

Spread the filling between two cookies, sandwich style. Refrigerate them until the chocolate sets, about ten minutes. Store them in airtight containers at room temperature for up to five days, or store them in the refrigerator if the filling starts to melt.

Makes about 12 large cookies

MOCHIES

When I was growing up, we had a big brown Labrador retriever named Mocha, more commonly referred to as Mochie. I used to make these brownies in honor of him, and that's how the name evolved.

1 cup (2 sticks) butter
4 ounces unsweetened chocolate
1 tablespoon instant coffee powder
4 eggs
Pinch of salt
1½ cups sugar
½ cup all-purpose flour
⅔ cup chopped walnuts

Heat the oven to 350°F. and grease a 9 × 13-inch baking pan.

Melt the butter and the chocolate in the top of a double boiler over a low flame, stirring constantly until the mixture is well combined. Add the coffee powder, stirring to dissolve it. Let the mixture cool.

Beat the eggs, salt and sugar with an electric mixer until thick and creamy, about 3 minutes. Gently fold in the chocolate mixture and mix lightly until just incorporated. Do not overbeat or the eggs will deflate. Carefully fold in the flour and then the walnuts.

Pour the batter into the prepared pan and bake for 25 minutes or until the center is barely firm. These cookies are ready even before a tester inserted in the center comes out clean, and in order to maintain their chewiness it is important not to overbake them. Watch them carefully.

Cool the cookies in the pan on a rack and then cut them into squares. Store them in airtight containers in the refrigerator for up to four days.

Makes 28 bars

CAPPUCCINO BALLS

These crunchy cookies are not as sweet as they are rich. They make an important contribution to a dessert buffet, but are equally perfect with steaming cup of their namesake on a quiet afternoon.

1 **cup toasted hazelnuts**
1 **ounce bittersweet chocolate**
½ **cup (1 stick) butter at room temperature**
pinch of salt
¼ **cup granulated sugar**
1 **tablespoon milk**
1 **tablespoon instant espresso powder**
1 **cup all-purpose flour**
½ **cup confectioner's sugar**
2 **teaspoons cinnamon**
1 **teaspoon finely ground espresso beans**

In a food processor or blender, finely grind the hazelnuts and the chocolate. Set aside.

With an electric mixer, cream the butter with the salt and sugar until the mixture is light and creamy, about 1 minute.

In a small saucepan over low heat, or in a microwave, gently scald the milk (that is, heat until small bubbles appear around the edges of the pan; do not boil). Remove the pan from the heat and mix in the espresso powder until it is thoroughly dissolved. Add it to the butter mixture and stir well. Gradually add the hazelnut mixture and the flour, mixing lightly until just incorporated. Do not overmix or the crumb will toughen. The dough may be used immediately or refrigerated, tightly wrapped, for up to three days.

Heat the oven to 325°F. and line two baking sheets with parchment or wax paper.

Shape the dough into 1-inch balls, and place them about ½ inch apart on the prepared baking sheets. Bake until firm and lightly colored, about 15 minutes.

While the cookies are baking, whisk together the confectioner's sugar, cinnamon, and ground espresso beans.

With a spatula, transfer the cookies to a wire rack. When

they are cool enough to handle, carefully roll them in the confectioner's sugar mixture. Store them in airtight containers at room temperature for up to one week.

Makes about 35 cookies

MOCHA CRISPS

Crunchy cookies with an exquisite flavor and a sweet icing. They are just the thing for the holidays, and look especially winning if you use a pastry bag fitted with the smallest tip to decorate each cookie with the glaze. The sweet ground chocolate is available by mail order from Williams-Sonoma and Dean & DeLuca (see Sources).

For the Cookie Dough:
  1 cup (2 sticks) butter
  ¾ cup granulated sugar
  2 tablespoon sweet ground chocolate
  2 tablespoons cold brewed espresso
  ½ teaspoon coffee extract
2½ cups all-purpose flour
  ¼ teaspoon salt
  ½ teaspoon baking soda
  ¼ cup coffee flavored liqueur

For the Glaze:
  2 tablespoons soft butter
  ¼ cup coffee liqueur
  1 cup confectioner's sugar

Cream butter and sugar with an electric mixer until fluffy and light, about 1 minute. Beat in the chocolate, espresso, and coffee extract. Sift together the flour, salt, and baking soda, and gradually add them in three additions, alternating with the coffee liqueur, which should be added in two additions. Stir until the mixture is just combined. Refrigerate the dough, well wrapped, for at least four hours, and up to three days. You may also freeze the dough.

Heat the oven to 350°F. Line two cookie sheets with parchment or wax paper.

Divide the dough into quarters and work with one piece at a time, keeping the rest in the refrigerator until needed. Using as little flour as possible, roll the dough to a scant ⅛ inch. Cut with a two-inch round cookie cutter, place on the prepared baking sheets at least ½ inch apart, and bake for 8 to 10 minutes, until they are just set. Cool on a wire rack.

While the cookies are cooling, make the glaze. Beat the butter, liqueur, and confectioner's sugar in a small bowl until smooth and glossy. Use a small espresso spoon or a ⅛-teaspoon measure to drop the icing onto the cooled cookies. When the icing is completely dry, store the cookies in airtight containers at room temperature for up to three days.

Makes about 50 cookies

MOCHA CHEWS

These cookies are my favorite to serve at any special buffet. Adults love them for their tiny grace and intense flavor, while children love the fudgy texture. Actually, come to think of it, everyone loves the fudgy texture. Make these often and you will find yourself surrounded by admirers.

2 ounces unsweetened chocolate, chopped
5 tablespoons butter
2 eggs
1 cup granulated sugar
2 teaspoons coffee extract
1 cup all-purpose flour
1 teaspoon baking powder
⅛ teaspoon salt
Confectioner's sugar for rolling the dough in

Combine the butter and chocolate in the top of a double boiler, over simmering water, and stir until they are melted. Let cool.

Beat the eggs, sugar, and coffee extract together until smooth. Add the chocolate mixture and combine well.

Sift together the flour, baking powder, and salt. Gradually add to the chocolate mixture, mixing lightly until just incorporated. Do not overmix or the crumb will toughen. Refrigerate the dough, well wrapped, for at least 30 minutes, and up to three days.

Heat the oven to 350°F. Lightly grease several baking sheets.

Shape the dough into ¾-inch balls, roll in confectioner's sugar, and place cookies about ½ inch apart on the prepared baking sheets. Bake for about 8 minutes; they will look underbaked, but this is okay. Cool cookies on the baking sheet for 5 minutes, then transfer to a wire rack and cool completely. Store in airtight containers at room temperature for up to one week.

Makes about 24 cookies

ORANGE ESPRESSO BARS

I have been using a recipe for Snoopy Lemon Bars, which I found in The Peanuts Gallery Cookbook, *for over fifteen years. By substituting orange for the lemon and adding brewed espresso, I created this most fortunate variation.*

For the Crust:
½ cup (1 stick) butter
1 cup confectioner's sugar
2 cups all-purpose flour
1 tablespoon grated orange zest
¼ teaspoon salt

For the Filling:
4 eggs
2 cups granulated sugar
¼ cup cold brewed espresso
1 teaspoon coffee extract
1 tablespoon grated orange zest
¼ cup all-purpose flour
¼ teaspoon baking powder
Confectioner's sugar (optional)

Heat the oven to 350°F. Line a 9 × 13-inch baking pan with wax paper.

Place all of the ingredients in a food processor and pulse until they are just combined and still crumbly.

Evenly press the crust mixture into the prepared baking pan. Bake until light brown, 20 to 25 minutes.

To make the filling: beat the eggs and sugar with an electric mixer until thick and creamy, about 3 minutes. Blend in the espresso, coffee extract, and orange zest. Sift together the flour and baking powder, and gently fold into the egg mixture.

Pour the filling onto the crust, and bake for 30 minutes. Cool completely before cutting into bars. Store in airtight containers in the refrigerator for up to four days. For appearance' sake, you may want to dust these with confectioner's sugar before serving.

Makes about 30 bars

BISCOTTI

Biscotti are definitely all the rage. As good coffee becomes more and more popular, so do these crunchy cookies, which are lovely to dip into your steaming mug of brew. Originally biscotti were generally made with nuts and spices, but today's cookies contain everything from chocolate to dried fruit to black pepper and wine.

The word biscotti, in Italian, means "twice cooked," which is exactly the way these biscuits are made. First, the dough is shaped into a log and baked. When it is cool enough to handle, the log is sliced and baked again, making for a dry and crisp texture that absorbs liquid like a sponge. In slower times, biscotti were perfect for long overseas journeys where fresh food was not available, because they kept very well. If they lasted that long, that is. Today their keeping properties make them just the thing for mailing as gifts, packed into decorative tins.

In addition to coffee-dipping, biscotti are wonderful plunged into sweet wine. With a selection of fresh fruit, this combination produces a traditional and elegant Italian dessert.

WALNUT ORANGE BISCOTTI

Made with butter, these biscotti are unusually rich. The grated orange peel really perks up the flavor.

  2 cups all-purpose flour
  ½ teaspoon baking soda
  ½ teaspoon baking powder
  ¼ teaspoon salt
  ⅔ cup unsalted butter at room temperature
  1 cup sugar
  2 eggs
Grated zest of two large oranges
  2 teaspoons vanilla extract
1½ cups coarsely chopped toasted walnuts

Heat oven to 350°F. and grease two baking sheets.

Sift together flour, baking soda, baking powder, and salt. Set aside.

With an electric mixer, beat the butter and sugar until light and creamy, about 2 minutes. Add the eggs, one at a time, beating well after each addition. Mix in the orange zest and vanilla extract. Carefully mix in the dry ingredients, beating only until they are just incorporated. Overbeating will toughen the crumb. Fold in the nuts.

Shape the dough into a long thin log, or make two shorter logs. Place the logs on one of the prepared baking sheets and bake for 20 minutes. Remove from the oven and cool to room temperature.

Using a serrated bread knife, cut the logs into 1-inch slices. Place them cut side down on the other greased cookie sheet and bake for 20 minutes, until golden brown.

Place the cookie sheet on a rack and let the biscotti cool completely. Store them in airtight tins for three or more weeks.

Makes about 20 biscotti

BLACK PEPPER–ALMOND BISCOTTI

These cookies are traditionally free of shortening and have a very dry, hard, but delightful texture. They are my favorite dippers because they don't fall apart as easily as others. Try them with sweet wine to gracefully end an Italian meal.

  4 **cups all-purpose flour**
  2 **cups sugar**
  2 **teaspoons baking powder**
  2 **teaspoons freshly ground black pepper**
  6 **eggs**
  ¼ **cup cognac**
  2 **teaspoons almond extract**
  2 **teaspoons vanilla extract**
  2 **cups coarsely chopped toasted almonds**

Heat the oven to 350°F. Grease two baking sheets.

In a food processor, process the flour, sugar, baking powder, and pepper until they are well mixed, about 10 seconds. Add the eggs consecutively through the feed tube while the machine is running. Then add the cognac, the almond extract, and the vanilla extract and process until the mixture comes together in a dough. Add the nuts, and pulse on and off until just combined.

Shape the dough into a long, thin log or make two shorter logs. Place the logs on one of the prepared baking sheets and bake for 20 minutes. Remove from the oven and cool to room temperature.

Using a serrated bread knife, cut the logs into 1-inch slices. Place them cut side down on the other greased cookie sheet, and bake for 20 minutes, until they are golden brown.

Place the cookie sheet on a rack and let the biscotti cool completely. Store them in airtight tins for three or more weeks.

Makes about 20 biscotti

RED WINE–ANISE BISCOTTI

This unusual combination is utter harmony when eaten alongside a strong espresso. Dipping is optional with these beauties, which taste just as nice dry. Use any type of nut you happen to have or use a combination.

1 tablespoon anise seeds
1¼ cups (2½ sticks) unsalted butter at room
      temperature
1½ cups sugar
6 eggs
6 cups all-purpose flour
1 tablespoon baking powder
1½ teaspoons salt
¼ cup dry red wine
3 cups coarsely chopped toasted nuts

Heat the oven to 350°F. Grease two baking sheets.

Using a mortar and pestle or a spice grinder or food processor, pound or grind the anise seeds just enough to release their scent. Set aside.

With an electric mixer, cream the butter and sugar until light and fluffy, about 2 minutes. Add the anise seeds and beat well.

Beat the eggs in a separate bowl until they are slightly foamy. Sift the flour with the baking powder and salt, and add, alternately with the eggs, to the butter mixture, beating between each addition and scraping the sides of the bowl with a rubber spatula. Gently mix in the wine and nuts.

Shape the dough into a long, thin flat log or make two logs. Place the logs on one of the prepared baking sheets and bake for 20 minutes. Remove from the oven and cool to room temperature.

Using a serrated bread knife, cut the logs into 1-inch slices. Place them cut side down on the other greased cookie sheet, and bake for 20 minutes, until they are golden brown.

Place the cookie sheet on a rack and let the biscotti cool completely. Store them in airtight tins for three or more weeks.

Makes about 20 biscotti

HAZELNUT-CINNAMON BISCOTTI

These spicy biscuits are sensational in the cooler months when cappuccino beckons. For a toothsome variation, dip half of each cookie into melted choco-

*late and let dry on a rack. When they are swirled into
hot coffee, some of the chocolate melts into the liquid,
making mocha, while the chocolate still coating the
cookie gets warm and soft like fudge. Indulge yourself!*

½ cup (1 stick) unsalted butter at room temperature
1 cup sugar
½ teaspoon salt
1 teaspoon cinnamon
Finely grated zest of ½ an orange
3 eggs
3 cups all-purpose flour
2½ teaspoons baking powder
½ teaspoon baking soda
2 cups coarsely chopped toasted, skinned hazelnuts

Heat the oven to 325°F. Grease two baking sheets.

With an electric mixer, cream the butter, sugar, salt, cinnamon, and orange zest until light and creamy, about 1
minute. Add the eggs one at a time, beating well after each
addition.

Sift the flour, baking powder and baking soda together
and fold into the batter. Do not overmix or the crumb will
toughen. Fold in the nuts.

Shape the dough into a long log or make two logs. Place
the logs on one of the prepared baking sheets and bake for
25 minutes. Remove from the oven and cool to room temperature.

Reduce oven temperature to 275°F. Using a serrated
bread knife, cut the logs into 1-inch slices. Place them cut
side down on the other greased cookie sheet, and bake for
50 minutes, until they are golden brown.

Place the tray on a rack and let the biscotti cool completely. Store them in airtight tins for three or more weeks.

Makes about 20 biscotti

DELICATE PIGNOLI BISCOTTI

These wonderful cookies are much thinner and smaller than the other biscotti in this book. Pignoli nuts add a distinctly Italian flavor, however untraditional they may seem in biscotti. If you prefer, you can substitute almonds.

½ cup (1 stick) unsalted butter at room temperature
¾ cup sugar
2 whole eggs
1 egg yolk
2 tablespoons dry Marsala
2¼ cups all-purpose flour
1½ teaspoons baking powder
½ teaspoon salt
½ cup lightly toasted pignoli

Heat the oven to 325°F. Generously grease two baking sheets.

With an electric mixer, cream the butter with the sugar until light and fluffy, about 2 minutes. Add the eggs and egg yolk one at a time, beating well after each addition. Beat in the Marsala.

Sift together the flour, baking powder, and salt. Gradually add to the batter and mix only until incorporated. Do not overmix or the crumb will toughen. Fold in the nuts.

Shape the dough into three or four long, thin logs, about an inch in diameter, and place them on the baking sheets at least two inches apart. Flatten them slightly. Bake for 25 minutes. Remove from the oven to cool on a rack for ten minutes or until cool enough to work with.

Using a serrated bread knife, cut the rolls into ½ slices, and lay them cut side down on the same baking sheets. Bake for 15 minutes, until dry and golden brown. Store them in airtight containers for three or more weeks.

Makes about 50 biscotti

CHOCOLATE ALMOND BISCOTTI

These traditional tiny cookies hail from Venice, where almonds, chocolate, and dried fruits are favorite flavorings for crunchy biscotti.

    1 cup toasted almond slices
 2½ cups all-purpose flour
  ¾ cup sugar
  ⅛ teaspoon salt
    1 teaspoon baking soda
    2 eggs
    1 egg yolk
  ¾ cup semisweet chocolate chips
    1 egg white

Heat oven to 375°F. Grease two baking sheets.

In a food processor, finely grind one-third of the almonds, one tablespoon of the flour, and one tablespoon of the sugar until powdery. Do not overprocess. Add the remaining flour and sugar, and process to combine, about 10 seconds. Add the salt and the baking soda and pulse to mix.

With the motor running, add the eggs and egg yolk through the feed tube. Process until just combined. Add the chocolate chips and the remaining almonds and pulse lightly.

Divide the dough into four pieces and shape each piece into a thin log. Place two rolls on each baking sheet. Beat the egg white until frothy and brush it on the rolls. Bake for 20 minutes, remove from oven and cool for ten minutes.

Lower oven to 225°F. With a serrated bread knife, cut the logs into ½-inch diagonal slices. Place the slices cut side down on the same baking sheets and bake for 30 minutes. Remove from oven, cool, and store in airtight containers for three or more weeks.

Makes about 40 biscotti

MOM'S PECAN RUM BISCOTTI

Although this is not a traditional Italian recipe, I made these biscotti at my mother's suggestion, and they were wonderful dippers. Something about the mingling flavors of rum and coffee produce a very fragrant evening nibble.

½ cup (1 stick) **unsalted butter at room temperature**
1 cup **sugar**
½ teaspoon **salt**
Finely grated zest of 1 lemon

   2 whole eggs
   1 egg yolk
   3 tablespoons dark rum
   3 cups all-purpose flour
2½ teaspoons baking powder
   ½ teaspoon baking soda
   2 cups coarsely chopped toasted pecans

Heat the oven to 325°F. Grease two baking sheets.

With an electric mixer, cream the butter, sugar, salt, and lemon zest until light and creamy, about 1 minute. Add the eggs and egg yolk one at a time, beating well after each addition. Beat in the rum.

Sift the flour, baking powder, and baking soda together and fold into the batter. Do not overmix or the crumb will toughen. Fold in the nuts.

Shape the dough into a long log or make two logs. Place on one of the prepared baking sheets and bake for 25 minutes. Remove from the oven and cool to room temperature.

Reduce oven temperature to 275°F. Using a serrated bread knife, cut the logs into 1-inch slices. Place them cut side down on the other greased cookie sheet and bake them for 50 minutes, until they are golden brown.

Place the tray on a rack and let the biscotti cool completely. Store them in airtight tins for three or more weeks.

Makes about 20 biscotti

GOLDEN RAISIN BISCOTTI

The raisins in this recipe are first soaked in a grappa, a clear Italian spirit distilled from the skins and pips of grapes after they are pressed for wine. The grappa plumps up the raisins and adds punch to the cookies. If you don't have any grappa on hand, brandy will work just fine, as will French marc or any other dry liqueur. Just choose your favorite, and this biscotti will surely become one of your favorite recipes.

    2 cups golden raisins
    ¼ cup grappa, brandy, or another dry liqueur
    1¼ cups (2½ sticks) unsalted butter at room
        temperature
    1½ cups sugar
    6 eggs
    6 cups all-purpose flour
    1 tablespoon baking powder
    1½ teaspoons salt
    1 cup coarsely chopped toasted almonds

The night before you want to make the biscotti, place the raisins in a small bowl, pour the grappa over the raisins, and let sit, stirring occasionally. The raisins will absorb the liquid and fatten up.

Heat oven to 350°F. Grease two baking sheets.

With an electric mixer, cream the butter and sugar until light and fluffy, about 2 minutes.

Beat the eggs in a separate bowl until they are slightly foamy. Sift the flour with the baking powder and salt and add, alternately with the eggs, to the butter mixture, beating between additions and scraping the sides of the bowl with a rubber spatula. Gently mix in the raisin-grappa mixture and the nuts.

Shape the dough into a long log or make two logs. Place the logs on one of the prepared baking sheets and bake for 20 minutes. Remove from the oven and cool to room temperature.

Cut the logs into 1-inch slices. Place them cut side down on the other greased cookie sheet, and bake for 20 minutes, or until golden brown.

Place the tray on a rack and let the biscotti cool completely. Store them in airtight tins for three or more weeks.

Makes about 20 biscotti

CHOCOLATE CHERRY BISCOTTI

These biscotti are not as sinful as they sound; they are demure, sophisticated little treats that I make in miniature to serve with candied orange peel at the end of a great meal or as a very elegant coffee break. Dried sour cherries are available at specialty shops around the country as well as by mail order from American Spoon Foods (see Sources).

⅓ cup toasted almond slices
2½ cups all-purpose flour
¾ cup sugar
⅛ teaspoon salt
1 teaspoon baking soda
2 eggs
1 egg yolk
¾ cup semisweet chocolate chips
⅔ cup dried sour cherries
1 egg white

Heat the oven to 375°F. Grease two baking sheets.

In a food processor, finely grind the almonds with one tablespoon of the flour and one tablespoon of the sugar until powdery. Do not overprocess or you will have almond butter. Add the remaining flour and sugar, and process to combine, about 10 seconds. Add the salt and baking soda and pulse to mix.

With the motor running, add the eggs and egg yolk through the feed tube. Process until just combined. Add the chocolate chips and the cherries, and pulse lightly.

Divide the dough into four pieces, and shape each piece into a thin log. Place two logs on each baking sheet. Beat the egg white until frothy, and brush on the rolls. Bake for 20 minutes, remove from the oven and cool for ten or so minutes.

Lower oven to 225°F. Using a serrated bread knife, cut ½ inch slices on a diagonal from the logs. Place the slices, cut side down, on the same baking sheets and bake for 30 minutes. Remove from oven, cool and store airtight for three or more weeks.

Makes about 40 biscotti

CAKES AND PIES

CAPPUCCINO POUND CAKE

This is unquestionably the best pound cake I have ever had. It melts instantly in your mouth leaving a rich coffee-cinnamon sensation behind. The basic recipe is from Rose Levy Beranbaum's The Cake Bible, *but I have adapted it slightly and flavored it differently. I used six egg yolks in this recipe because I had them on hand after testing a nonfat mocha cake, which is not in this book because it bounced back too strenuously when I tried to cut it. If you prefer, use three whole eggs instead, as the original recipe suggests.*

   1 tablespoon sugar
   2 teaspoons cinnamon
   3 tablespoons milk
   1 tablespoon instant coffee granules
   6 egg yolks
   1 teaspoon vanilla extract
1⅓ cups cake flour
 ¾ cup sugar
 ¾ teaspoon baking powder
 ¼ teaspoon salt
13 tablespoons unsalted butter at room temperature

Heat oven to 350°F. Grease and flour an 8 × 4 × 2½-inch loaf pan.

In a small bowl, combine the 1 tablespoon sugar with the cinnamon.

In a medium bowl mix the milk and instant coffee until the coffee is dissolved. Add the egg yolks and vanilla and stir.

With an electric mixer, combine the flour, the ¾ cup sugar, the baking powder, and the salt, and mix on low speed for 30 seconds to blend. Add the butter and half of the egg mixture and mix on low speed until the ingredients are moistened. Increase to medium speed and beat for 1 minute. Scrape the sides with a rubber spatula. Gradually add the remaining egg mixture in 2 batches, beating for 20 seconds after each addition and scraping the sides.

Scrape the batter into the prepared pan and smooth the surface with a spatula. Sprinkle with cinnamon-sugar mixture. Bake 55 to 65 minutes, or until a toothpick inserted in the center comes out clean. Cover loosely with buttered foil after 30 minutes to prevent overbrowning.

Cool the cake in the pan on a rack for 10 minutes, and then remove from the pan and cool completely.

DARK MOCHA LOAF CAKE

This cake is like a pound cake, but it is moister, richer, and studded with chocolate chips and nuts. It freezes particularly well, makes a delightful gift, and is all an all-around crowd pleaser.

  1 **egg**
1½ **cups sour cream**
 ¾ **cup light brown sugar**
  6 **tablespoons (¾ stick) unsalted butter, melted and cooled**
1½ **cups all-purpose flour**
  1 **teaspoon salt**
1½ **teaspoons baking soda**
 ½ **cup unsweetened cocoa**
 ¼ **cup espresso powder**
  1 **cup chocolate chips**
 ½ **cups coarsely chopped toasted walnuts**

Heat oven to 350°F. Grease and flour a 7-cup or larger capacity loaf pan.

Beat the egg, sour cream, and brown sugar until well mixed. Beat in the melted butter. Sift together the dry ingredients and add to the egg mixture, stirring until just incorporated. Stir in the chocolate chips and the nuts.

Pour the batter into the prepared pan and smooth the top. Bake for 55 to 65 minutes, or until a cake tester inserted in the center comes out clean.

Cool the cake in the pan on a rack for 10 minutes; then unmold it and cool completely. Serve immediately, or wrap in plastic and store in the refrigerator for up to three days. The cake cuts better and, to me, tastes better, when it is cold.

MOIST MOCHA CAKE

This cake is sublime in its simplicity. No fancy icings, add-ons, or fillings mar its purity. For a very special party, you may lightly dust the surface with confectioner's sugar, but even without it, this cake will reign over the gilded many.

10 ounces bittersweet chocolate, broken into pieces
¾ cup (1½ sticks) unsalted butter
1 cup sugar
3 tablespoons instant coffee granules
5 egg yolks
⅓ cup cake flour
5 egg whites
Powdered sugar for dusting (optional)

Heat the oven to 350°F. Butter a 9-inch cake pan.

Combine the chocolate, butter, and sugar in the top of a double boiler over barely simmering water, and stir until the chocolate melts. Mix in the instant coffee and let cool.

Whisk the egg yolks into the chocolate mixture. Whisk in the flour.

Beat the egg whites just until they form stiff peaks when the mixer is lifted. Be careful not to overbeat.

Add one-third of the egg whites to the chocolate mixture and mix well. Carefully fold in the remaining whites, mixing only until they are incorporated and no streaks of white are visible in the batter. Do not overmix.

Pour the batter into the prepared pan and bake until the cake is firm to the touch, 35 to 40 minutes. Cool thoroughly on a rack. Dust with the confectioner's sugar, if desired.

ESPRESSO NUT TORTE

This spicy cake offers an unusual combination of flavors and textures. Serve slivers with rich espresso after a light winter meal. The recipe is based on one given to me by an Italian friend, who says it is a traditional wedding cake passed down in her family for generations.

For the Cake:
1¼ cups toasted almonds
1¾ cups toasted and skinned hazelnuts
 1 tablespoon finely ground espresso beans
 8 eggs, separated
⅔ cup sugar
¼ teaspoon salt
½ teaspoon cream of tartar
 2 tablespoons unsalted butter, melted
¼ cup dark rum

For the Filling:
 8 ounces almond paste

For the Icing:
1½ cups heavy cream
1½ teaspoons coffee extract
 3 tablespoons confectioner's sugar

Heat the oven to 300°F. Grease and flour two 9-inch cake pans.

In a food processor grind the almonds, hazelnuts, and espresso beans until they are finely ground. Do not overprocess.

Beat the egg yolks with half of the granulated sugar until the mixture is thick and syrupy. In a separate bowl beat the egg whites with the salt and cream of tartar until they hold soft peaks. Add the rest of the sugar and beat until very stiff peaks form and the whites look glossy.

Mix the butter and rum into the egg yolks. Fold one-quarter of the egg whites into the yolks to lighten them. Carefully, so the whites do not deflate, fold in the rest of the yolk mixture. Gently fold in the nuts.

Scrape the batter into the prepared pans and bake for 40 to 45 minutes, or until a cake tester inserted in the center of the cake comes out clean. Remove from oven and sprinkle each layer with half of the rum. Cool the cakes in the pans on a rack.

When the cakes are completely cool, unmold one layer onto a serving plate and prepare the filling: roll out the almond paste between two sheets of wax paper until it forms approximately an 8 ½-inch circle. Place the circle of almond paste on top of the unmolded cake layer. If the almond paste tears, just patch it together. Unmold the second layer directly on top of the almond paste. The bottom of the second layer should be the top of the cake.

To make the icing: whip all of the ingredients together until the mixture is thick and fluffy. Ice the cake and serve that same day.

MOCHA SOUFFLÉ CAKE WITH COFFEE BUTTERCREAM

A classically luscious, creamy cake made with al-monds and bittersweet chocolate and coated with coffee-flavored buttercream. I like to make this cake for coffee-lovers' birthdays, decorating it with icing swirls and rosettes and mocca beans. You can make the cake the day before you plan to ice it; just wrap well and refrigerate overnight.

For the Cake:

  4 egg yolks
  ¾ cup granulated sugar
  6 ounces bittersweet chocolate
  ¾ cup (1½ sticks) unsalted butter
  3 tablespoons instant coffee granules
  4 tablespoons cake flour
  2 tablespoons ground almonds
  4 egg whites
  ⅛ teaspoon salt

For the Icing:

  ¾ cup confectioner's sugar
  4 tablespoons (½ stick) unsalted butter at room
      temperature
  2 tablespoons instant coffee granules dissolved in
  2 tablespoons hot water, cognac, or dark rum
Mocca beans (optional)

Heat the oven to 375°F. Butter and flour an 8-inch cake pan. Line the bottom with a piece of wax paper cut to fit. Butter the waxed paper.

Beat the egg yolks and the granulated sugar until the mixture is thick and creamy. Melt the chocolate and the butter in the top of a double boiler over simmering water, stirring until smooth. Add the instant coffee and stir to dissolve the granules. Whisk in the egg yolk mixture, and lightly beat until well blended. Stir in the flour and the almonds. Remove the double boiler from the heat.

Beat the egg whites with the salt until stiff, glossy peaks form. Do not overbeat. Mix one-quarter of the egg whites into the chocolate mixture to lighten it. Gradually fold in the rest of the whites, mixing until just combined. Take care not to deflate them. If your double boiler top is too small to accommodate the rest of the egg whites, you may add the chocolate mixture to the bowl of egg whites. Just be extra cautious as you fold.

Turn the batter into the prepared pan and smooth the top. Bake for 22 to 25 minutes, or until the center of the cake is set and does not jiggle when you gently shake the pan. The cake will still be slightly wet and creamy, so do not insert a cake tester. Do not overbake this cake, or it will dry out.

Cool the cake in the pan on a rack. Unmold onto a serving dish.

To make the icing: combine all of the ingredients in a bowl and beat until the mixture is thick and creamy. Spread on the cake and decorate to your taste. Top with mocca beans, if you like.

COFFEE PISTACHIO ROULADE

This ethereal cake will please everybody. It is moist and soft and highly sophisticated. Best of all, it's easy to make and you can freeze the whole thing for up to one month, if you need to. You can substitute walnuts or hazelnuts for the pistachios.

For the Cake:
 5 egg yolks
 ½ cup granulated sugar

Pinch of salt
  1 tablespoon coffee extract
1¼ cups ground pistachios
  ½ teaspoon baking powder
  5 egg whites

For the Filling:
  ½ cup milk
  3 tablespoons finely ground coffee
1½ cups ground pistachios
  1 cup heavy cream
  ½ cup unsalted butter at room temperature
  ⅔ cup granulated sugar
  2 tablespoons cognac
Confectioner's sugar

Heat the oven to 375°F. Spray an 11 × 17-inch jelly roll pan with cooking spray; or dot it with butter, line it with wax paper, and grease the paper.

Beat the egg yolks with the granulated sugar, coffee extract and salt until light and creamy. Add the pistachios and baking powder and mix to combine.

Beat the egg whites until they are stiff and glossy. Do not overbeat. Gently fold them into the yolk mixture. Spread the batter in the prepared pan and bake for 15 minutes, or until a cake tester inserted the center comes out clean. Cover the cake with a damp kitchen towel and let it cool on a rack.

To make the filling, heat the milk until tiny bubbles appear around the sides of a saucepan; remove from heat. Stir in the coffee and let mixture seep for ten minutes. Strain the milk through a cheesecloth-lined sieve into a bowl, and add the walnuts. Let the mixture cool.

Whip the cream and set aside. In a mixing bowl, cream the butter and the sugar until light and fluffy, about 2 minutes. Beat in the cooled nut mixture and the cognac. Gently fold in the whipped cream.

Sprinkle the cake with confectioner's sugar. Spread a long strip of wax paper on the countertop. Invert the cake onto the paper and peel the wax paper from what was the bottom of the cake. Spread the filling evenly on the cake, and use the wax paper to help you roll it up like a jelly roll. Cover well and refrigerate up to three days. Sprinkle with more confectioner's sugar before serving.

TOFFEE ESPRESSO CREAM CAKE

Crunchy and creamy, this sinful cake is made of two espresso-flavored sponge layers sandwiching buttery toffee and coffee-flavored whipped cream. It is meltingly tender and rich and an utter treat.

For the Cake:
 3 egg yolks
 1 cup sugar
 ¼ cup freshly brewed espresso
Pinch of salt
 1 cup cake flour
 1 teaspoon baking powder
 3 egg whites

For the Filling:
¾ cup coffee toffee (page 179), finely chopped
 1 recipe Crème Chantilly au Café (page 193)

Heat the oven to 350°F. Butter and flour two 9-inch cake pans.

Beat the egg yolks with ¾ cup of the sugar until thick, creamy and pale, about 5 minutes. Add the espresso and salt and mix well.

Sift together the salt, flour, and baking powder. Gradually add to the yolk mixture, stirring until just incorporated. Do not overbeat.

Beat the egg whites until they are very foamy but still soft. Add the remaining ¼ cup sugar and beat until the mixture is stiff but not dry. Gently fold one-quarter of the whites into the yolk mixture to lighten it. Then fold in the remaining whites, being careful not to deflate them. Scrape the batter into the prepared pans and smooth the tops.

Bake for 20 minutes, or until the top springs back when lightly pressed. Cool the cakes in the pans on a rack for 5 minutes; then unmold and cool completely.

Prepare the filling: Mix ⅔ cup chopped toffee with 1 cup of the whipped cream. Spread this on one layer and top with the other one. Ice the cake with the remaining whipped cream and then sprinkle on the remaining toffee decoratively. Serve immediately or refrigerate for up to 8 hours. The cakes may be wrapped in plastic and stored in the refrigerator for two days. Fill and ice as close to serving time as possible.

OLD-FASHIONED SPICE CAKE

Brimming with dried fruit and spices and capped with a silken frosting, this tender cake is lovely during the holiday season. It also keeps well, and even improves after a few days.

For the Cake:

- ½ cup dark raisins
- ½ cup golden raisins
- ½ cup coarsely chopped prunes
- ½ cup coarsely chopped dried apricots
- ⅓ cup strong brewed coffee
- 1 cup (2 sticks) unsalted butter at room temperature
- 1 cup packed dark brown sugar
- 1 cup granulated sugar
- 4 eggs
- 3¼ cup all-purpose flour
- 2 teaspoons baking powder
- 1 teaspoon baking soda
- 1 teaspoon cinnamon
- 1 teaspoon ground cardamon
- ½ teaspoon nutmeg
- ½ teaspoon ground cloves
- ½ teaspoon salt
- 1¼ cups plain yogurt
- 1 teaspoon vanilla extract

For the Icing:

- ½ cup unsalted butter at room temperature
- 8 ounces cream cheese, room temperature
- 2 teaspoons coffee extract
- 4 cups confectioner's sugar

Place the raisins, prunes, and apricots in a small bowl with the coffee and let the fruits soak for at least one hour or overnight.

Heat oven to 350°F. Grease and flour two 9-inch cake pans.

Cream butter, the brown sugar, and the granulated sugar together until the mixture is fluffy. Add the eggs, one at a time, beating well after each addition. Sift together the dry ingredients and the spices and gently fold them into the batter, mixing until just incorporated. Mix the yogurt, vanilla extract, and dried fruit–coffee mixture together, and fold into the batter, being careful not to overmix, but making sure everything is amalgamated.

Scrape the batter into the prepared pans and bake for 35 to 40 minutes, or until the cake springs back when the center is lightly touched. Cool the cakes in the pans on a rack for 10 minutes; then unmold and cool completely.

To make the icing: cream the butter, cream cheese, and coffee extract until smooth. Add the confectioner's sugar and beat until smooth. Ice the cake and serve at once, or wrap well and store in the refrigerator for up to three days.

COFFEE-CHESTNUT EXTRAVAGANZA

Coffee and chestnuts go very well together as their individual spicy, earthy flavors complement one another perfectly. In this dessert, two rum-scented yellow cake layers enclose a coffee-flavored chestnut puree and are frosted with a billowy chestnut-coffee cream. Crowned with a ring of marrons glacés, this makes a very fancy, equally succulent cake. Crème de marrons and marrons glacés are available at specialty food shops, and by mail from Dean & Deluca and La Cuisine.

For the Cake:

¾ cup (1½ sticks) unsalted butter at room
     temperature
1½ cups sugar
 1 cup whole milk
 2 teaspoons vanilla extract
 6 egg yolks
 3 cups cake flour
½ teaspoon salt
 1 tablespoon baking powder
¼ cup dark rum

For the Filling:

 1 cup crème de marrons
 1 tablespoons coffee extract

For the Icing:

½ cup crème de marrons
 1 tablespoon rum
 1 teaspoon instant espresso (powdered or granular)
 1 cup heavy cream
12 marrons glacés (optional)

Heat the oven to 350°F. Grease and flour two 9-inch cake pans.

With an electric mixer, cream the butter and the sugar until the mixture is light and fluffy, about 2 minutes. Scrape the sides of the bowl. In a separate bowl, stir together the milk, vanilla, and egg yolks.

Sift together the flour, salt, and baking powder. Add about one-third of the dry ingredients to the butter and sugar mixture and stir to combine. Then add half of the egg mixture, and all of the rum and stir well. Continue in this vein, scraping the sides as necessary, until everything is combined and smooth. Do not overmix.

Scrape the batter into the prepared pans and bake for 25 to 35 minutes or until a tester inserted into the center comes out clean. Cool the cakes in the pans on racks for 10 minutes, then unmold and cool completely.

To make the filling: Mix together the crème de marrons and the coffee extract. Spread this on one of the cake layers. Top with the other layer.

To make the icing: Combine the crème de marrons, rum, and espresso in a small bowl. In a medium bowl, whip the cream until it is thick but still soft. Add the chestnut mixture and beat until stiff. Ice the cake prettily, making rosettes and swirls with a pastry bag if you are good at it. Top with marrons glacés if you have them and serve that day.

MOCHA-GLAZED BANANA CAKE

This is a simple, lush cake that makes an ideal snack. While I love to eat it for breakfast, the rest of my household seems to prefer it at teatime. Whatever times we all choose, it never lasts more than one day. Use very ripe bananas with black spots all over the skin; otherwise the cake will not have a strong enough flavor.

For the Cake:
- 1 cup (2 sticks) unsalted butter at room temperature
- ¾ cup sugar
- 2 eggs
- 1 teaspoon vanilla extract
- 1 tablespoon hot water
- 1 tablespoon instant coffee granules
- ¼ cup molasses
- 3 very ripe bananas, mashed with a fork
- 2¼ cups all-purpose flour
- 1½ teaspoons baking soda
- ½ teaspoon salt
- ½ cup sour cream

For the Glaze:
- 12 ounces bittersweet chocolate
- 1⅔ cups sour cream
- 2 tablespoons instant espresso (powdered or granular)

Heat the oven to 350°F. Grease and flour two 9-inch cake pans.

With an electric mixer, cream the butter and the sugar until the mixture is light and fluffy, about 2 minutes. Add the eggs, one at a time, beating well after each addition.

In a small bowl mix the vanilla extract, hot water, and instant coffee, stirring until the coffee dissolves. Pour this to the butter and sugar mixture and mix well. Add the molasses and bananas and beat for 20 seconds to combine.

Sift together the flour, baking powder, and salt and add half to the batter, mixing until just combined. Add the sour cream and then the rest of the flour, beating gently after each addition. Do not overmix.

Scrape the batter into the prepared pans and bake for 30 to 35 minutes or until a toothpick inserted in the center comes out clean. Cool the cakes in the pans on a rack for 10 minutes; then unmold and cool completely.

To make the glaze: Chop the chocolate into small pieces, and melt it in a double boiler over barely simmering water, stirring frequently. Remove from heat and stir in the sour cream and espresso powder, mixing until smooth. Spread on cake while glaze is still warm.

MOCHA PRALINE CHIFFON PIE

This pie is just light enough not to seem as rich as it is. The praline adds a delightful crunch to the smooth, cloudlike mocha filling. Although the recipe seems complicated, each step is really quite simple. This pie is not difficult to prepare, but it is time-consuming, so plan ahead.

For the Filling:
- 6 tablespoons (¾ stick) unsalted butter
- ½ cup packed dark brown sugar
- ½ cup finely chopped pecans
- 1 package unflavored gelatin
- ¼ cup hot water
- 4 egg yolks
- ⅓ cup unsweetened cocoa
- 1¼ cups granulated sugar
- ¼ teaspoon salt
- 1 cup strong hot coffee
- 4 egg whites
- ½ cup cream

Mocca beans or chocolate shavings

For the Crust:
1½ cups all-purpose flour
½ teaspoon salt
½ cup (1 stick) cold unsalted butter cut into small pieces
¼ cup ice water

Make the crust: Place the flour and salt in a food processor and process just to combine. Add the butter and pulse on and off until the mixture looks like coarse meal and there are no large lumps of butter. With the motor on, add the ice water and process until a ball begins to form.

Turn the dough out onto the counter top, knead it for a few seconds, and then put it into a large, flat circle. Wrap in plastic and refrigerate for at least 1 hour and up to 3 days.

Heat the oven to 425°F.

On a floured board, roll the pie crust dough into an 11-inch circle. Place in a 9-inch pie tin and crimp the edges decoratively. Prick all over the bottom with the tines of a fork. Line the crust with a sheet of foil, and weigh down the foil with pennies, dried beans, rice, or pie weights to prevent air bubbles from forming. Bake for 10 minutes.

While the crust is baking, melt the butter and brown sugar in a small saucepan over medium heat, stirring constantly until the mixture boils vigorously. Remove from heat and stir in the pecans.

Remove piecrust from oven and remove the foil and pie weights. Spread in the nut mixture. Return the crust to the oven and bake for 5 more minutes. Cool completely on a rack.

Sprinkle the gelatin over the hot water and let sit 5 minutes. Beat the egg yolks until they start to thicken. Mix the cocoa, ½ cup of the granulated sugar and the salt in a small bowl. Pour in the coffee and stir until the sugar is dissolved. Add this mixture to the egg yolks and mix well.

Transfer the egg yolk mixture to a medium saucepan and cook over low heat, stirring constantly, until the custard coats the spoon. Do not let the mixture boil.

Remove the custard from the heat and strain it into a clean bowl. Add the softened gelatin, stir well, and let the custard sit at room temperature until it is completely cool. Then refrigerate until it thickens to the consistency of mayonnaise.

While the custard is chilling, beat the egg whites until they are foamy. Then gradually add the rest of the sugar and beat until the whites are stiff and glossy, but not dry. Fold one-quarter of the egg whites into the custard to lighten it, then carefully fold in the rest. Do not let the whites deflate. Pour the filling into the baked pie shell, mounding it in the center. Refrigerate until cold.

Just before serving, whip the heavy cream until thick. Spread it, or pipe it with a pastry bag, onto the pie. Decorate with the mocca beans or chocolate shavings and serve immediately.

COFFEE-SCENTED BAKLAVA

Although the Greeks love coffee, it is rare to find it incorporated into their pastry. However, do not let this stop you from trying this superlative recipe. It will really impress anyone you serve it to. Phyllo dough is available frozen at most supermarkets. You may substitute walnuts for the pistachios, if you wish. Baked baklava freezes beautifully.

For the Pastry:

 4 cups finely chopped pistachios
 ⅔ cup sugar
 1 teaspoon ground cinnamon
 ¼ teaspoon ground cloves
1½ pounds phyllo dough
 2 cups (4 sticks) unsalted butter, melted

For the Syrup:

 2 cups sugar
 1 cup mild honey
 1 cup strong brewed coffee
 2 cinnamon sticks, each about 3-inches long
 4 whole cloves
 1 tablespoon grated orange zest
 1 teaspoon orange flower water

Heat the oven to 350°F. Butter a 12×7 ½×2-inch baking pan.

To make the pastry: In a small bowl mix the nuts, sugar, cinnamon, and cloves.

On a countertop, lay out the phyllo dough and cover it with a plastic wrap and a damp towel so it won't dry out while you are working. With a pastry brush, brush one sheet of phyllo with melted butter. Place the sheet, butter side up, across one end of the pan; there should be a bit of overhang on three sides, with the fourth side lying flat in the center of the pan. Butter another sheet and lay this one next to the other, so that it covers the other end of the pan. Layer another 9 sheets, buttered on one side on top of the first two. Keep the stack of unused phyllo leaves covered at all times so they will not dry out. If the butter starts to congeal, place it over a pan of simmering water until it melts again.

Once you have layered 10 leaves of phyllo, sprinkle the

top with about ⅔ cup of the nut mixture, and top with another 10 leaves of phyllo layered in the same fashion. Sprinkle with another ⅔ cup of nuts, and continue layering nuts and phyllo until all the filling is used up. Layer the remaining phyllo leaves, painting them with butter as you go. The last leaf should have the butter facing up. Brush the phyllo hanging over the sides of the pan with butter, and roll it up so the rolls sit nicely on top of the pastry, acting like a border. With a very sharp knife, cut *only* through the top layers of the phyllo, making three vertical cuts and four horizontal cuts to form twelve squares. Then cut each square in half on the diagonal, resulting in 24 triangles. Sprinkle the surface with a few drops of warm water.

Bake for 50 minutes, or until the top is a deep golden color.

While the baklava is baking, make the syrup: Simmer together all of the ingredients in a saucepan for 10 minutes. Strain the syrup and let it cool.

When the baklava is ready, remove it from the oven and set it on a rack to cool. Pour half of the syrup evenly over it, and let it cool for 20 minutes. Then pour the rest of the syrup on and let it cool completely. It is best to prepare the baklava at least one day in advance.

WHITE CHOCOLATE–KAHLÚA CRUNCH CHEESECAKE

I adapted this voluptuous cheesecake from a recipe in the Silver Palate Good Times Cookbook, *and it has been a standard in my repertoire ever since. It is as dense and creamy as they come, so serve skinny slices with bracing black coffee for a delectable combination. This is an ideal dessert to make ahead of time, even for your fanciest dinner parties.*

Make sure the white chocolate you use has cocoa butter as one of the ingredients, or the resulting cake will taste slightly greasy and bland. Tobler and Callebaut are my favorites, with Lindt and Valrhona coming in a close second. You can order any of these from Dean & Deluca or La Cuisine.

½ **pound crisp, plain cookies**
½ **teaspoon very finely ground coffee**
¼ **cup toasted pecans**
2 **tablespoons brown sugar**
13 **tablespoons unsalted butter at room temperature**
1 **pound imported white chocolate, finely chopped**
2 **pounds cream cheese at room temperature**
4 **whole eggs**
1 **egg yolk**
¼ **cup Kahlúa**
¾ **cup crushed coffee-flavored toffee (see page 179)**

Heat the oven to 300°F. Thickly butter a 9-inch or 10-inch springform cake pan.

In a food processor combine the cookies, coffee, pecans, and brown sugar, and process until everything is finely crushed. Melt 5 tablespoons of the butter and process into the crumb mixture. Press it onto the sides and bottom of the prepared pan and refrigerate.

In the top of a double boiler over hot water, melt the white chocolate, stirring constantly. White chocolate burns very easily, so be patient and never let the water underneath it boil.

With an electric mixer, beat the cream cheese until light and fluffy, about 2 minutes. Beat in the whole eggs and the egg yolk, one at a time, and then the remaining butter (which is not melted) and the white chocolate. Mix in the Kahlúa, and then the toffee. Carefully pour this mixture into the crumb crust.

Bake for 1½ hours, or until the center is set. Cool completely on a rack, and then chill thoroughly before serving.

PAIN D'ÉPICE

This wonderfully aromatic spice cake happens to be traditionally virtually fat-free, so you can encourage seconds without guilt. Plan to start this cake the week before you want to serve it. Once baked, it keeps getting better, so it's a good dessert to have on hand for the unexpected guest.

  1 **cup freshly brewed hot coffee**
  1 **cup honey**
  ¼ **cup sugar**
  ¼ **teaspoon salt**
  2 **teaspoon baking soda**
  ½ **teaspoon baking powder**
  ½ **cup rum**
  1 **teaspoon finely ground aniseed**
  1 **teaspoon cinnamon**
  ½ **teaspoon ground ginger**
  ¼ **teaspoon ground cloves**
  ½ **teaspoon powdered mustard**
  ¼ **teaspoon finely ground black pepper**
1¾ **cups rye flour**
1¾ **cups all-purpose flour**
  ¼ **cup very coarsely chopped candied orange peel**
  ⅓ **cup currants or raisins (optional)**
  ½ **cup coarsely chopped blanched almonds**

In a large bowl, mix the coffee and honey until the honey is melted and the mixture is smooth. Stir in the sugar, salt, baking powder, and baking soda, and then the rum and aniseed.

Sift together the spices and flours and add them gradually to the honey mixture, beating only until smooth and lump-free. Mix in the orange peel, and currants or raisins if you are using them.

Cover the bowl tightly with plastic wrap, and refrigerate the batter for at least three days and up to a week. This will intensify and marry the flavors, and help refine the texture.

Heat the oven to 400°F. Grease and flour two 8 × 4-inch loaf-pans. Add the almonds to the batter and mix well. Scrape into the prepared pans. Bake the cakes for 10 minutes, then lower the oven temperature to 350°F. Bake for 50 minutes, or until a cake tester inserted into the center comes out clean.

Cool the cakes in the pans on a rack for 15 minutes, then unmold and cool completely. If you would like to glaze these cakes, melt some jelly or honey in a saucepan, and brush it on the tops. You can also decorate the tops with almonds, orange peel and the like. Wrap the cakes tightly in plastic and let them sit undisturbed in the refrigerator for a few days. They just keep getting better.

RICOTTA COFFEE TART

This is a pleasantly light coffee-flavored Italian cheesecake variant. It is not too sweet and makes a lovely end to any meal.

For the Crust:
 1 **cup all-purpose flour**
 ¼ **cup sugar**
Pinch of salt
 1 **egg yolk**
 2 **teaspoons vanilla extract**
 1 **tablespoon milk**
 4 **tablespoons (½ stick) cold unsalted butter, cut into
       pieces**

For the Filling:
1½ **cups ricotta cheese**
 1 **whole egg**
 4 **egg yolks**
 1 **cup Coffee Syrup, boiled with a 3-inch piece of
       cinnamon stick (see page 189)**
Finely grated zest of 1 lemon

Heat the oven to 375°F.

Make the crust. In a food processor, process the flour, sugar, and salt until combined. Add the egg yolk, vanilla, and milk and pulse on and off until to mix. Add the butter and process until the dough starts to clump together.

Turn the dough out onto a floured work surface and shape it into a disk. With you hands, gently press the dough into a 9-inch tart pan. Prick the bottom all over with the tines of a fork and line the inside with foil. Fill the foil with pennies, dried beans, rice, or pie weights to prevent bubbles from forming. Bake for 20 minutes and then remove the foil. Lower oven temperature to 350°F. and bake for another 10 minutes, or until the crust is pale golden brown. Cool thoroughly on a rack.

Raise the oven temperature to 375°F.

In a bowl whisk together the ricotta, the whole egg and

the egg yolks, the coffee syrup, and the lemon zest until very smooth. Pour the mixture into the tart shell and bake for 35 to 45 minutes, or until the top is golden brown. The center will still seem a bit runny, but it will firm up as it cools.

Remove the tart from the oven and cool completely.

CARAMELIZED FIG TART

This rich dessert is complicated in flavor only; it is really quite simple to prepare, and it's one of the most beautiful confections I have ever put together. Enjoy it accompanied by a special dessert wine and share it with special friends.

Tart dough for a 9-inch crust (see Ricotta Coffee Tart, page 148)
1 pound fresh purple figs at room temperature
1 cup sugar
⅓ cup water
Few drops of lemon juice
1 teaspoon coffee extract
Whipped cream (optional)

Heat the oven to 375°F. Line a 9-inch tart pan with the rolled-out pie dough and decoratively crimp the edges. Cover the pastry with foil and fill with pennies, dried beans, rice, or pie weights to prevent bubbles from forming. Bake for 20 minutes and then remove the foil. Lower oven temperature to 350°F and bake for another 10 minutes, or until the crust is golden brown. Cool thoroughly on a rack.

Trim the stemmed tops off each fig, cutting far enough down so some of the bright red center shows through. Arrange them concentrically in the pie shell and set aside.

In a small, heavy (preferably enameled) saucepan combine the sugar, water, and lemon juice and let the mixture sit until the sugar is moistened. Cook over medium heat, gently swirling the pan, just until the caramel turns a light golden brown. Immediately remove the pan from the heat and swirl in the coffee extract. Carefully pour the caramel over the figs, taking care that it falls in a thin, even coat. Do not let it start to clump in one area.

Let the caramel cool until it turns brittle and glassy, and then serve the tart immediately. It is best to make this tart on a dry day; otherwise the caramel will get sticky. If you must make it in humid weather, assemble it as close to serving time as possible. In dry weather the tart will keep at room temperature for several hours. Serve with whipped cream, if desired.

MOCHA MADELEINES

I'm sure Proust never dreamed of this variation on his nostalgic little cakes. Although they are too moist and strongly flavored for dunking in tilleul, try eating them alongside a dry dessert wine or with a glass of port or by themselves. In texture and flavor you will find them reminiscent of very rich chocolate cake, made small enough to be eaten out of hand.

This recipe is based upon one by Joel Robuchon, the renowned French chef reigning at Jamin in Paris. Patricia Wells has collected many of his recipes in her book Simply French, *a most fitting tribute to Robuchon's genius.*

  13 tablespoons unsalted butter
   5 ounces imported bittersweet chocolate, chopped
1⅔ cups confectioner's sugar
  ½ cup plus 1 tablespoon all-purpose flour
  ½ cup ground almonds
  6 egg whites
  1 tablespoon mild honey
  2 tablespoon instant espresso (powdered or
       granulated)

Grease and flour 2 madeleine tins (for about 24 cakes).

In a large saucepan, melt the butter over medium-high heat. In about 5 minutes, the foam in the butter will begin to darken and turn golden brown. Immediately transfer the butter to a medium-size bowl.

Melt the chocolate in the top of a double boiler over, but not touching, simmering water. Stir constantly until it is smooth and remove from heat. Let cool.

Sift together the confectioner's sugar and flour, and then stir in the almonds.

In the bowl of an electric mixer, beat the egg whites until they are foamy. Add the flour mixture and whisk until they are combined. Add the honey and the instant espresso to the butter and stir well. Then add this mixture to the eggs. Add the melted chocolate and gently stir until the batter is well blended.

Spoon the batter into the prepared molds, filling them ¾ full. Refrigerate for about 50 minutes to firm them up.

Heat oven to 375°F.

Bake the madeleines until they are springy to the touch. Remove them from the oven and rap the pans on the countertop to loosen the cakes. Unmold them immediately, using the tip of a small, sharp knife, if necessary. Set on a rack to cool. You can store them in an airtight tin for a few days, but they are best eaten that day.

TIRAMISU

This luscious Italian creation features coffee-soaked cookies layered with thick marscapone cheese (available at specialty cheese shops and some large supermarkets). The name means "pick-me-up," which with all that coffee it certainly is. Serve it in the afternoon rather than after dinner, or warn your guests of the possible caffeine ramifications. Or make it with decaf. This is a nice dessert to make in the summer since it is very elegant but requires no cooking. It keeps very well, although it never lasts long enough. Serve small squares; it is rich.

3 cups very strong hot coffee
¼ cup Sambuca
½ cup plus 1 tablespoon sugar
2 whole eggs
2 egg yolks
2 cups marscapone cheese
1 cup heavy cream
2 packages anisette sponges or Italian ladyfingers
1 cup grated bittersweet chocolate

In a small bowl, stir together the coffee, the Sambuca, and 1 tablespoon of the sugar until the sugar is dissolved.

With an electric mixer, beat the eggs and egg yolks, the remaining ½ cup sugar, and the marscapone until light and fluffy. In another bowl, whip the cream until it is very thick. Gently fold the cream into the marscapone mixture. Do not overmix.

Working quickly, dip each cookie into the coffee. Do not let the cookies absorb too much of the liquid or the cake will be mushy. Arrange one layer of cookies on the bottom of a glass baking dish or a shallow bowl. Top with 1 cup of the marscapone cream, then with another layer of cookies. Continue in this fashion until both are used up.

Cover the top with the grated chocolate. Refrigerate the tiramisu for several hours or overnight.

HONEY-GLAZED APPLE ESPRESSO PIE

A very fragrant old-fashioned pie with a modern twist. You can substitute pears or quinces for the apples. To make the dough, you can double the Mocha Praline Chiffon Pie recipe (page 141).

Pie dough for two 9-inch crusts
¼ cup honey
 1 tablespoon instant espresso (powdered or
      granulated)
 6 tart cooking apples, peeled, cored, and very thinly
      sliced
⅓ cup sugar
½ teaspoon salt
 1 teaspoon cinnamon
 3 tablespoon all-purpose flour
 2 tablespoons butter, cut into very small pieces
Milk

Heat the oven to 375°F.

Roll out half the pastry dough on a lightly floured surface and line a 9-inch pie plate with it. Wrap the other half in plastic and refrigerate until needed.

In a small saucepan, melt the honey until it is liquid. Remove from heat and stir in the instant espresso. In a large bowl, toss the honey mixture with the apple slices until the slices are well coated.

Sift together the sugar, salt, cinnamon, and flour and lightly toss them with the apples until they are evenly coated.

Pour the apple filling into the prepared pie pan and dot with the butter.

Roll out the reserved pastry into an 11-inch circle, and cover the pie with it. Crimp the edges decoratively and cut three air vents in the center. Brush the crusts with milk.

Bake for 40 to 60 minutes, or until the apples are tender and can be easily pieced with a fork. If the crust starts to get too brown, cover loosely with foil.

Remove the pie from the oven and cool completely on a rack.

FROZEN DESSERTS

Although coffee is usually best enjoyed steaming hot, the sultry summer weather often precludes this fix. This is the perfect time to take your coffee in another form, namely frozen. Granitas and sorbets are frozen flavored coffee, while the ice creams are richer fare. Sample them all because, before you know it, hot coffee season will arrive with the first fallen leaves.

GRANITA DI CAFFÈ

This is the purest way to take your coffee frozen, because that is all it is. The best part about it is the chunky, ice texture, which melts on your tongue like snowflakes and really cools you down on a steaming day. If you want to dress it up for a dinner party, make Granita di Caffè con Panna, and layer the ice with either the Crème Chantilly au Café (page 193) or, as I prefer it, with plain, unsweetened whipped cream. The contrast in flavors is quite striking.

To vary the basic recipe, add some grated orange or lemon peel and maybe a bit of orange juice to the coffee mixture before you freeze it, or add some cinnamon, ginger, or clove for a spicier twist.

Sugar to taste
1 quart freshly brewed strong hot coffee
Pinch of salt
Whipped cream or Crème Chantilly au Café (page
193) (optional)
Mocca beans, chocolate shavings, or mints leaves
(optional)

Mix as much sugar as you like in the hot coffee until it dissolves. Add the salt and stir. Cool to room temperature.

Transfer mixture to a loaf or baking pan, made of metal. (If you use a glass pan, your granita will not freeze, because glass is not a good temperature conductor, and won't get cold enough. Similarly, the shallower the pan you use, the more surface area you expose to the cold air in your freezer, and the quicker the mixture will freeze.)

Freeze the coffee for two hours, stirring well every half hour to break up the ice crystals. The texture should resemble ice shavings and be a little firmer than slush. If you need to hold the granita, you can, for another two hours or so, and break up the ice in your food processor directly before serving. If you leave it longer than this, it will freeze up solid like a giant ice cube, and be impossible to work with.

To serve, scoop some of the granita into a wineglass or serving bowl, and then spoon on a layer of cream, if you are using it. Top with more granita and more cream, and decorate with mocca beans, chocolate shavings, or mint springs, if desired. Serve immediately.

Makes about 1 quart

GRANITA DI CAFFÈ E CIOCCOLATA

A chocolate-spiked version of the preceding recipe,
this granita has a full flavor without the heaviness of
chocolate in the summertime.

 3 cups freshly brewed strong hot coffee
Pinch of salt
Sugar to taste
½ cup grated or finely chopped bittersweet chocolate
½ cup fresh raspberries (optional)

Combine the hot coffee with the salt, sugar, and chocolate. Stir until most, but not all, of the chocolate is dissolved.

Transfer the mixture to a metal loaf or baking pan and
freeze for two hours, stirring well every half hour to break
up the ice crystals. The texture should resemble ice shavings and be a little firmer than slush. Hold the granita for
another two hours or so, if necessary, and break up the ice
in your food processor directly before serving. If you leave
it longer than this, it will freeze up solid like a giant ice
cube and be impossible to work with.

Serve immediately in wineglasses or parfait dishes, garnished with fresh raspberries, if desired.

Makes about 1 quart

JULIAN CLARK'S MOCHA SORBET

A sorbet differs from a granita in its texture, which is
smooth and creamy as opposed to icy. You will need
an ice cream maker for this wonderful recipe, which

was created by my father. It is very elegant served by itself, ungarnished, or in a tuile cookie cup. You may never go back to eating chocolate ice cream again.

2 cups freshly brewed, very strong hot coffee
7 ounces bittersweet chocolate, finely grated
1 cup sugar
Pinch of salt

In the top of a double boiler, place the hot coffee, the chocolate, the sugar, and the salt. Stir until the chocolate and sugar melt completely and the mixture becomes syrupy and homogenous. If the coffee cools before the mixture is fully melted, place the pan over, but not touching, the bottom half of the double boiler filled with simmering water. Stir until smooth and satiny.

Chill the mocha mixture until it is completely cooled. Freeze in an ice cream maker according to manufacturer's instructions.

Makes 3 cups

COFFEE CUSTARD ICE CREAM

This is an extremely rich ice cream best served in small portions. To cut the richness, serve it with some hot espresso poured right on top. The hot and bitter liquid melting into the cold, creamy ice cream is fabulous, if you like contrast as much as I do. Or gild the lily by serving this ice cream drowned in Espresso Fudge Sauce (page 191). You may never recover, but what a way to go!

 3 cups heavy cream
¾ cup sugar
¼ cup freshly roasted, coarsely ground coffee beans
 6 egg yolks
 1 teaspoon vanilla extract

In a medium-sized saucepan, heat the cream until tiny bubbles appear around the edges of the saucepan. Stir in the the sugar until it dissolves. Remove from heat.

Add the ground coffee beans and let sit for ten to twenty minutes, tasting, until the taste pleases you. Strain well through a fine sieve lined with cheesecloth, into a clean saucepan. Return the mixture to heat and warm slightly.

Beat egg yolks until well combined. Add a little of the warm coffee mixture to the eggs, stirring constantly, to bring up their temperature so they won't curdle when added to the custard.

Stirring the custard constantly with a wire whisk, slowly add the tempered eggs to the pan, and cook over low heat until the custard coats the back of a spoon. Do not let the mixture boil.

Strain the custard through a fine sieve to remove any lumps, and stir in the vanilla extract. Cool in the refrigerator until it is thoroughly chilled, and freeze it in an ice cream maker according to the manufacturer's instructions.

Makes about 1 quart

PUDDINGS AND SOUFFLÉS

CRÈME BRÛLÉE AU CAFÉ

This is a wonderful way to enjoy crème brûlée. Finely ground coffee is sprinkled over the custard before it bakes. The grounds sink to the bottom, leaving a coffee-flavored trail amid the vanilla pudding with its crackling caramel crust.

  1 **plump, moist vanilla bean**
  1 **cup whole milk**
1½ **cups heavy cream**
  3 **egg yolks**
  2 **whole eggs**
 ¼ **teaspoon salt**
 ¼ **cup granulated sugar**
1–2 **teaspoons very finely ground coffee beans**
Light brown sugar for sprinkling on the top

Heat the oven to 300°F.

Slit the vanilla bean lengthwise down its center. Combine the milk, cream, and vanilla bean in a medium-sized saucepan. Bring just to a boil and remove from heat. Let the mixture steep for fifteen minutes.

161

While the cream is steeping, whisk together the egg yolks, whole eggs, salt, and sugar. Then add a little of the cream mixture to the eggs to warm them, whisking constantly. Pour the tempered eggs into the pot with the cream and cook over medium heat, stirring constantly with a wooden spoon until the custard thickens enough to coat the spoon. Do not let the mixture boil. Strain the custard into a clean bowl. (The custard may be made up to four days in advance. Store in tightly covered in the refrigerator.)

Divide the custard amongst 6 half-cup ramekins. Sprinkle a small pinch of the coffee onto each cup. Arrange the ramekins in a large baking pan, and fill the pan halfway with very hot water. Be careful not to spill any water into the custards.

Bake for 30 to 40 minutes, until the center is set and a sharp knife inserted into the center comes out clean. Remove custards from the pan to a rack, and let them cool for 20 minutes. Then cover them tightly with plastic wrap and refrigerate for 2 to 4 hours.

Just before serving, sprinkle a thin layer of brown sugar on each custard. Run them under the broiler until the sugar melts and caramelizes, about 2 minutes. Watch them carefully, because the sugar can go from caramelized to burned in seconds. Serve the custards immediately.

Serves 6

CARAMELIZED ESPRESSO-CHESTNUT SOUFFLÉ

This excellent recipe has always been a favorite of mine, and with the addition of coffee it takes on an even greater depth. The caramel is first swirled inside the baking dish, then the soufflé is scraped on top. The whole is baked and left to cool. Unmolded, the caramel forms a syrupy sauce complementing the airy, mousselike soufflé underneath. You can buy whole peeled chestnuts at specialty shops and large supermarkets, especially near the holiday season.

1 cup whole milk
1 cup heavy cream
4 tablespoons espresso coffee, medium grind
1 pound whole peeled chestnuts
1 cup sugar
Dash of salt
2½ tablespoons water
3 egg whites
Whipped cream for garnish (optional)

Heat the oven to 325°F. Place a round ceramic baking dish or cake tin with a 6-cup capacity next to the stove.

In a small, heavy saucepan, bring the milk and cream just to a boil, remove the pan from the heat, and add the ground coffee. Let the mixture steep for 15 minutes. Then strain it through a cheesecloth-lined sieve into a large saucepan.

Add the chestnuts, ¾ cup of the sugar, and salt to the milk mixture and simmer for 30 minutes, or until the chestnuts are tender. Let the mixture cool for a few minutes, and then puree it in a food processor, in several batches if necessary.

In a clean, small heavy saucepan combine the water with the remaining ¼ cup sugar. Heat the mixture over a medium flame, gently shaking the pan occasionally, until the sugar caramelizes and turns golden brown. Immediately remove the pan from the heat and pour the caramel into the baking pan, swirling it until the caramel coats the bottom and at least halfway up the sides.

Beat the egg whites until they are glossy and stiff, but not dry. Fold about one-third of the whites into the chestnut mixture to lighten it, and then gently fold in the rest, taking care not to deflate the eggs. Scrape the mixture into the caramelized baking dish.

Place the soufflé dish in a large baking pan and fill the pan halfway up with very hot water. Make sure none of the water drops on the soufflé. Carefully transfer the pan to the oven and bake for 40 to 50 minutes, or until the center does not jiggle much when you shake it. Immediately turn the soufflé onto a serving dish, and let it cool. Serve cold with whipped cream, if you like.

COFFEE HAZELNUT SOUFFLÉS WITH COGNAC SAUCE

These individual soufflés are simultaneously light and rich, and utterly wonderful to savor. While not difficult to prepare, they do call for patience, and they must be made at the last minute. The sauce, however, can be made a few days in advance, and it is just as nice to eat with coffee ice cream.

1 cup whole milk
3 tablespoons coffee, medium grind
3 egg yolks
⅓ cup sugar
Pinch of salt
2 tablespoons all-purpose flour
2 tablespoons unsweetened cocoa
¼ cup finely chopped toasted and skinned hazelnuts
3 egg whites
1 recipe for Coffee-Cognac Sauce (page 194)

In a small, heavy saucepan, heat the milk and the coffee until the milk just boils. Remove the pan from the heat and let the coffee steep for 15 minutes.

Meanwhile, beat the egg yolks with the sugar and salt until they are thick and creamy, about 3 minutes. Sift the flour and cocoa into the egg yolks and mix to combine.

Strain the milk, and add a little of it to the egg yolks, stirring constantly. Add the tempered egg yolk to the saucepan with the rest of milk, and cook over medium heat, stirring constantly with a wooden spoon, until the mixture thickens enough to coat the back of the spoon. Do not let the mixture boil.

Pour the custard into a medium-large bowl and let it cool until warm to the touch. Stir in the hazelnuts.

Heat the oven to 425°F. Butter 4 half-cup ramekins.

Beat the egg whites until they hold soft peaks when the beaters are raised. Gently fold about one-third of the egg whites into the cooled custard to lighten it, and then fold in the rest until just incorporated. Be careful not to deflate the whites.

Spoon the mixture into the prepared ramekins and bake

the soufflés for 15 minutes. They will be browned and puffed, but still jiggly in the center. Serve immediately with the cognac sauce.

Serves 6

MOCHA CINNAMON MOUSSE WITH TOASTED ALMONDS

Cool and spicy, this dense, autumnal mousse is a most welcomed indulgence.

 4 ounces bittersweet chocolate, grated
½ cup heavy cream
 3 tablespoons coffee, medium grind
Pinch of salt
½ cup sugar
 1 tablespoon cinnamon
 5 egg yolks
 1 tablespoon rum, cognac, or coffee-flavored liqueur
 5 egg whites
½ cup toasted almond slices

In the top of a double boiler, melt the chocolate over, but not touching, simmering water. Remove from heat and let cool.

In a saucepan bring the cream just to a boil and remove from heat. Add the coffee and let steep for 15 minutes. Using a cheese cloth-lined sieve, strain the cream into a clean medium saucepan. Stir in the salt, sugar, and cinnamon.

In a small bowl, beat the egg yolks until they begin to thicken, about 1 minute. Add a little of the hot cream to the yolk, stirring constantly, to warm them. Pour the tempered yolks into the rest of the cream mixture and cook over medium heat, stirring constantly, until the custard thickens enough to coat the back of a spoon. Do not let the mixture boil.

Remove the custard from the heat and stir in the melted and cooled chocolate. Let the mixture cool until warm to the touch. Stir in the liqueur.

Beat the egg whites until they are stiff and glossy but not dry. Fold about one-third of the whites into the custard to lighten it, and then fold in the rest until just incorporated. Be careful not to deflate the whites.

Spoon mousse into individual serving bowls; clear glass is particularly nice as it shows off the mousse's deep color. Refrigerate for at least 6 hours, or overnight. Garnish with the toasted almonds just before serving.

Serves 6

COFFEE-CARDAMOM PARFAIT

Coffee and cardamom have a wonderful affinity that is highlighted in this elegant dessert. Layers of deep, clear black coffee jelly and pale cardamom mousse make a striking and memorable presentation. Use fresh cardamom, either green or white, and remove the seeds from the pod shortly before using. This will give you the most intense flavor.

For the Jelly:
- 3 tablespoons sugar, or to taste
- 1 packet unflavored gelatin
- 3 cups freshly brewed strong hot coffee

For the Mousse:
- 1 packet unflavored gelatin
- ½ cup cold water
- 2 cups heavy cream, divided
- 1½ cups whole milk
- 1 teaspoon cardamom seeds, lightly crushed
- 1 cup sugar
- 3 egg yolks

Mocca beans or chocolate shavings for garnish

In a small bowl, stir the sugar and gelatin into the coffee until completely dissolved. Divide the mixture among six wineglasses and refrigerate them for about 3 hours.

While the jelly is setting, make the mousse. Sprinkle the gelatin over the cold water and let it soften for 5 minutes.

Heat 1 cup of the cream and all of the milk until it just boils. Remove from the heat and stir in the cardamom and sugar until well mixed.

Beat the egg yolks until they are slightly thick, about 1 minute. Add a little of the hot cream mixture to the yolk, stirring constantly, to warm them. Pour the tempered yolks into the rest of the cream mixture and cook over medium heat, stirring constantly, until the custard thickens enough to coat the back of a spoon. Do not let the mixture boil or you will have scrambled eggs.

Pour the custard into a large bowl, cover tightly with plastic wrap so that the plastic touches the surface of the pudding (to prevent a skin from forming) and chill for about 30 minutes, or until the custard has the consistency of a raw egg white.

Whip the remaining 1 cup cream until it is stiff. Fold about ⅓ of the whipped cream into the custard to lighten it, and then gently fold in the rest. Divide the mousse among the jelly-filled wineglasses and refrigerate for at least another 2 hours, or overnight. Serve garnished with mocca beans or chocolate shavings, and perhaps a crisp cookie.

Serves 6

FRUIT DESSERTS

FALL FRUIT COMPOTE WITH RED WINE AND COFFEE

This refreshing dish can be enriched with a dollop of whipped cream or a spoonful of coffee ice cream. Or serve it plain for a lighter but no less satisfying dessert. The whole thing can be made in advance and brought to room temperature before serving.

  2 cups red wine
  2 cups freshly brewed strong coffee
1½ cups sugar
  ½ unpeeled lemon, seeded and sliced thin
  1 three-inch cinnamon stick
  1 three-inch vanilla bean, split lengthwise
  4 cloves
  ⅛ teaspoon peppercorns
  1 bay leaf
  2 ripe bosc pears, peeled, cored, and cut in 2-inch chucks
  2 tart cooking apples (Granny Smith or mutsu), peeled, cored, and cut into 2-inch chucks
  6 Italian prune plums, halved and pitted

**½ cup dried fruit (apricots, figs, dates, raisins, or a
   combination)**
Mint leaves or grated lime peel (optional)
Whipped cream, ice cream, or yogurt (optional)

In a large pot or covered casserole combine the wine,
coffee, sugar, lemon, cinnamon, vanilla, cloves, peppercorns, and bay leaf and bring the mixture to a boil. Reduce
the heat and simmer the mixture for 15 minutes.

Add all of the fresh and dried fruit and poach in the
liquid until tender, 15 to 25 minutes. Different fruits will
have different cooking times, so remove the tender fruit
with a slotted spoon and transfer to a serving bowl.

Once all the fruit has been removed, raise the heat and
boil the liquid until it is thick and syrupy. Strain the syrup
through a fine sieve into a clean bowl and reserve until
serving time.

Place the fruit in a pretty serving bowl (clear glass is
especially nice). Pour some of the syrup over the fruit and
garnish with the mint or lime, and the whipped cream, ice
cream, or yogurt if you are using them. Serve the fruit with
the remaining syrup on the side. Crisp cookies make a nice
accompaniment.

Serves 6–8

COFFEE-POACHED SECKEL PEARS

*Seckel pears are like regular pears in miniature.
They have soft, almost translucent flesh, which is intensely flavored and sweet. Although it may seem
like a lot of work to peel and seed each tiny pear,
your reward will come when you present a bowl of*

these gems to your guests. The oohs and aahs seem like they'll never cease, but they do when the reverential silence of eating falls and quiets the room.

You can make these in advance; they benefit from a few days in the refrigerator. Sometimes I like to serve them with a crème Anglaise, just for variety's sake.

  2 pounds ripe Seckel pears, peeled, halved lengthwise, and seeded
  2 cups freshly brewed strong coffee
  ⅓ cup brown sugar
  1 three-inch cinnamon stick
  1 teaspoon cracked cardamom pods
Confectioner's sugar for garnish

In a large saucepan, combine the Seckel pears, the coffee, and enough water so the pears are covered completely by liquid. Gently bring the mixture to a boil, and stir in the brown sugar, cinnamon, and cardamom.

Reduce the heat and simmer the mixture, gently stirring occasionally to dissolve the sugar, until the pears are tender and easily pierced with a fork.

With a slotted spoon, transfer the pears to a bowl or container and reserve.

Bring the cooking liquid to a boil, and reduce the mixture until it is thick and syrupy. Strain it through a fine sieve and reserve until serving time. If you need to store the pears in the refrigerator for a few days, store the syrup separately.

To serve, divide the pears among six serving bowls and spoon some of the syrup on top. Garnish the pears with sifted confectioner's sugar, and serve immediately.

Serves 6–8

FRESH CHERRIES WITH ESPRESSO AND BRANDY

This dish embodies the very essence of summertime, when ripe cherries overflow from their containers in orchard stands and farmers' markets.

If you are fortunate enough to have access to the succulent white cherries known as Queen Anne's cherries, use them. They have a wonderfully complex flavor that works particularly well in this recipe. In any case, use only firm, ripe cherries with unblemished flesh. They hold the most flavor.

 2 **pounds ripe, sweet cherries, stemmed and stoned**
¼ **cup sugar**
 1 **tablespoon brewed espresso**
 1 **tablespoon brandy**

In a large skillet, combine the cherries and the sugar, and gently heat them over a low flame until the sugar starts to melt. Shake the pan frequently to distribute the juices.

Cook the cherries for a few minutes, until they are heated through and soft, but not mushy. Add the coffee to the skillet, and continue to shake the pan and cook the cherries for one more minute. Remove the pan from the heat.

Mix the brandy into the cherries, and transfer them and all their juices to a bowl or container to cool. When the cherries come to room temperature, chill them for at least one hour, and up to three days.

Serve the cherries cold or at room temperature, with their juices. Crisp cookies make a nice accompaniment.

Serves 6–8

ORANGE SALAD WITH WALNUTS, DATES, AND SPICED COFFEE SYRUP

This is a lovely winter dessert to eat after a rich meal. It is refreshing and sweet, but not cloying. Sometimes I like to add slices of ripe fresh pineapple, which add a lovely color and flavor contrast. Pomegranate seeds also add a pretty scarlet sparkle, and if you have the time and energy to pick apart a pomegranate, it is well worth the effort.

 6 navel or temple oranges, (any seedless variety
    will do)
¼ cup pitted and chopped dates
¼ cup toasted walnuts
½ cup Coffee Syrup (see page 189), made with
    cinnamon and cloves or other spices
Seeds of one pomegranate (optional)

With a shape knife, cut the peel off the oranges. To do this, first cut slices off the navel and stem ends of the orange so it can stand upright. Then trim away the peel on the sides, making sure to scrape off all the white, bitter pith. When all the oranges are peeled, slice them crosswise and place the slices on a pretty serving platter.

Sprinkle the chopped dates and toasted walnuts over the orange slices. Gently spoon the coffee syrup evenly over the platter.

Cover the platter lightly with plastic wrap and chill for at least 45 minutes.

Garnish with the pomegranate seeds and serve immediately, before they leach their color onto the oranges.

Serves 6

GINGERED CRANBERRY RELISH WITH COFFEE

A lovely Thanksgiving staple heightened by the addition of candied ginger, grapefruit, almonds, and coffee. Aside from making a very nice accompaniment to meats and poultry, this relish can also be baked into a piecrust for an unusual ending to an autumn meal.

 4 **cups cranberries**
½ **cup strong brewed coffee**
 1 **cup sugar**
 1 **small yellow grapefruit, peeled**
¼ **cup toasted walnuts**
 2 **tablespoons finely chopped candied ginger**

In a small saucepan, combine the cranberries, coffee, and sugar and gently bring the mixture to a boil over low heat. Let the berries simmer, stirring frequently, until they begin to pop. Immediately remove from heat. Transfer the cranberries to a bowl and let them cool.

While the berries are cooling, prepare the grapefruit by dividing it up into sections. Then with a sharp, small knife, peel away the membrane, surrounding the sections and discard the membrane and the seeds. Chop the sections into pieces and refrigerate, covered.

Add the walnuts and candied ginger to the cranberry mixture and gently stir to combine. Refrigerate, tightly covered.

An hour before serving time, take the cranberries and the reserved grapefruit pieces out of the refrigerator and allow them to come to room temperature.

Just before serving mix the grapefruit into the cranberry

mixture. Serve in a pretty glass bowl so your guests can appreciate the wonderful ruby color of this relish.

Makes about 5 cups

BANANAS FOSTER ESPRESSO

This recipe is a variation on the famous bananas Foster, which was invented at New Orleans's renowned Commander's Palace back in the 1950s. I have added a heady dose of espresso, which enlivens the dish with its rich, bitter flavor and caffeine jolt. Of course, you can use decaf.

Choose very ripe bananas to achieve maximum flavor in this dish. They should be deep yellow with black spots all over them, and smell like bananas. I usually buy underripe greenish-yellow bananas three days before I plan to use them. Kept on the counter in a fruit bowl or paper bag, they will ripen quite nicely. Contrary to popular belief, you can store ripe bananas in the refrigerator for a few days. The skin will turn black, but this will not affect their flavor. I like to use spiced rum in this dessert, but any dark rum will do.

 6 tablespoons unsalted butter
 4 ripe bananas, peeled, and halved lengthwise
 ½ cup brown sugar
 2 tablespoons brewed espresso
 2 tablespoons banana liqueur
 ⅓ cup dark rum
Freshly grated nutmeg
Coffee or vanilla ice cream (optional)

In a large skillet, melt the butter over a low flame. Add the bananas and sauté them for a minute or two. Add the brown sugar and the espresso, and continue to cook the bananas until they are soft and slightly golden brown.

Pour in the banana liqueur and the rum, and carefully ignite the alcohol with a match. It is nice to turn down the lights when you do this—a real show stopper.

Arrange two banana halves on each of four plates, with ice cream if desired, and spoon the sauce over it. Grate the nutmeg on top of the sauce, and serve immediately.

Serves 4

BLUEBERRY PLUM PRESERVES

Coffee was an inspired addition to this jam, which acquired a winy, complex flavor even from the small amount used. It has risen to the top of the jam list in my household, even supplanting loganberry as the new family favorite.

This recipe makes a small amount, which will probably be used up in a week. If you wish to make more, double or triple the recipe. You will, however, either have to freeze what you won't use within a week or can it in sterilized jars. Otherwise it will spoil.

1 cup blueberries, rinsed and picked over
½ cup plums, pitted and sliced
¼ cup strong brewed coffee
½ cup sugar, or more to taste
¼ teaspoon cinnamon (optional)
Lemon juice (optional)

In a medium-sized saucepan, combine the blueberries, plums, coffee, sugar, and cinnamon if you are using it, and simmer the mixture, stirring occasionally, until the sugar dissolves and the blueberries begin to pop and release their juice, about 5 minutes. Taste the mixture and add more sugar, if you wish. If it tastes too sweet, add a few drops of lemon juice. Use your judgment; jam-making is not an exact science.

Continue to cook the mixture until it thickens and looks like jam. This will probably take 10 to 15 minutes, but watch carefully.

When the preserves are thick enough to suit your taste, transfer them to a clean jar and cover tightly. Let the jam cool before storing it in the refrigerator.

Makes about 1½ cups

CANDIES

COFFEE TOFFEE PECAN

This is my favorite candy: rich, buttery caramel studded with pecans and crushed coffee beans. You could dip these candies in melted bittersweet or white chocolate for an even more decadent experience. Wrapped in colored cellophane, toffee always makes an appreciated gift, and it will keep for several weeks.

¼ cup water
1 cup granulated sugar
1½ cups packed light brown sugar
1 cup (2 sticks) unsalted butter
2 teaspoons vanilla or coffee extract
½ teaspoon baking soda
Pinch of salt
1½ cups coarsely chopped toasted pecans
1 cup lightly crushed coffee beans
Melted chocolate (optional)

Butter a 9×13-inch baking pan and place it by the stove. In a heavy medium-sized saucepan combine the water, the sugars, and the butter. Heat the mixture over a medium flame, stirring constantly, until it boils. Continuing to stir often, boil the caramel until it reaches 285°F. on a candy thermometer.

Remove the pan from the heat and stir in the vanilla or coffee extract, baking soda, salt, nuts, and coffee beans. Stir well to combine the ingredients.

Pour the candy into the baking pan and let it cool for about 5 minutes. Then, with a sharp knife or a razor blade, cut the candy about halfway to the bottom, without cutting all the way through, in horizontal and vertical lines to form the desired number of squares. Let the toffee cool completely.

When the toffee has cooled, carefully turn it out of the pan onto a cutting board or countertop. Flip it over and break the candy along the score marks. Dip into melted chocolate, if you wish, and store it in an airtight container for up to 3 weeks.

Makes about 1½ pounds

ESPRESSO TRUFFLES

One taster describes these velvety confections as "little balls of heaven." They are blissfully easy to prepare, will impress your guests when served with coffee after the dessert, and make wonderful gifts. As always, use the finest chocolate you can afford, such as Callebaut, Lindt, or Valrhona, all available by mail from La Cuisine and Dean & Deluca. An interesting variation on these would be to make them with white chocolate, inserting a whole coffee bean in the center. Everyone will love the surprise.

1½ cups heavy cream
  2 tablespoons unsalted butter
  2 tablespoons instant espresso (powdered or
      granular)
 12 ounces bittersweet chocolate, grated
1½ cups unsweetened cocoa
  ½ cup confectioner's sugar

In a small, heavy saucepan, heat the cream until it just boils. Remove from heat and stir in the butter, instant espresso, and chocolate until it is smooth and well combined.

Pour the mixture into a metal bowl or baking pan and refrigerate until the mixture is cold and firm. Do not be surprised if some of the cream separates and rises to the surface. This is okay; just proceed as usual.

Sift together the cocoa and confectioner's sugar, and reserve.

When you are ready to form the truffles, coat a melon-baller or a teaspoon with some of the cocoa mixture and scoop the truffle mixture into little balls. When all the balls have been scooped, coat your hands with cocoa and roll each ball between them to smooth the surface. Then dip the balls in the cocoa mixture, coating them well.

Store the truffles in an airtight container in a cool place or in the refrigerator for up to two weeks. They can also be frozen; just defrost them overnight in the refrigerator. They will last for three months in the freezer.

Makes about 35 truffles

TENDER COFFEE CARAMELS

These buttery caramels melt in your mouth with-out the stickiness of the firmer variety. If you would like to make an unctuous caramel sauce, simply re-move the candy from the heat a few minutes earlier and serve while it is still warm and runny.

  1 cup heavy cream
1¼ cups sugar
Pinch of salt
  ½ cup very mild honey
  1 teaspoon coffee extract
  1 tablespoon unsalted butter

Butter a 9×5-inch loaf pan and place by the stove.

In a small, heavy saucepan, heat the cream until it boils. Stir in the sugar, salt, and honey. Bring the mixture back to a boil and cook, stirring occasionally, for about 10 minutes or until a candy thermometer reads 257F°.

Remove the pan from the heat and stir in the coffee extract and the butter. Pour the candy into the loaf pan and let it cool completely. If the caramel feels too soft after it has cooled, scrape it back into the saucepan and boil it for another 2 minutes. It should be firmer now.

With a buttered knife, cut the caramel into squares, re-buttering the knife as necessary. Wrap the squares in plastic or wax paper, and store them in an airtight container in the refrigerator for up to two weeks.

Makes about 1 pound

MOCHA PISTACHIO FUDGE

A twist on good old-fashioned fudge, this creamy candy is worth every minute it takes to make. It travels very well, and I often send a batch to friends in Europe who cannot get fudge easily. It reminds them of home.

1 **cup half-and-half**
3 **ounces unsweetened chocolate, chopped or grated**
3 **cups sugar**
3 **tablespoons light corn syrup**
¼ **teaspoon salt**
3 **tablespoons unsalted butter**
2 **teaspoons coffee extract**
½ **cup pistachios**

Butter an 8-inch square pan and set it by the stove.

In a medium-sized, heavy saucepan heat the cream over a medium flame until it boils. Stir in the chocolate until it is melted, and then add the sugar, corn syrup, and salt, stirring to combine.

Continue to cook the mixture, stirring from time to time, until the sugar completely dissolves. Occasionally wipe the edges of the pan with a pastry brush dipped in cold water. This will remove any sugar crystals, which can ruin the texture of the fudge.

Once the sugar has melted, cook the mixture without stirring until it reaches 234°F. on a candy thermometer. Add the butter, but do not stir it in; just let it melt on top of the candy. Remove the pan from the heat and let the candy cool until it feels barely warm to the touch (110°F.).

When the fudge has cooled, add the coffee extract and

nuts and beat until the candy loses its gloss and begins to thicken. Quickly pour it into the prepared pan and let it cool completely.

Cut the fudge into squares and store it in an airtight container for up to three weeks.

Makes about 1½ pounds

COFFEE–PINE NUT PRALINES

These are sublime and sophisticated candies that everyone will adore. Wrap them in colored cellophane for a festive touch. You can substitute pecans for a more traditional candy.

1 cup heavy cream
2 cups light brown sugar
Pinch of salt
1 teaspoon coffee extract
2 cups toasted pine nuts

Line 3 or 4 baking sheets with wax paper and place them near the stove.

In a medium-sized, heavy saucepan, combine the cream, sugar, and salt and stir well. Cook over medium heat, stirring frequently, until the mixture reaches 236°F. on a candy thermometer. Immediately remove the pan from the heat.

Stir in the coffee extract and the nuts, and beat the mixture with a wooden spoon until it thickens and begins to sugar (turns white and grainy).

Drop the candies by tablespoons onto the wax paper.

Allow them to cool, and wrap them well in cellophane or wax paper. Pralines will keep for three weeks to one month when stored in airtight containers.

Makes about 1 pound

DESSERT SAUCES

These sauces can be used with other recipes in this book or to add a new dimension to any dessert already in your repertoire. Most of the recipes are drawn from the classical dessert sauce canon and then infused with coffee. I have included suggestions for using each one of these sauces, but of course you will probably come up with many others.

A reminder to the caffeine sensitive: all recipes in this book can be made with decaffeinated coffee, preferably not the water-processed kind.

COFFEE CRÈME ANGLAISE

This classic sauce has many, many variations, coffee being a particularly delicious one. Serve this sauce with fresh blueberries and plums, with chocolate pound cake, or on ice cream. Substitute another liqueur for the Kahlúa and invent your own sauce. Coffee has a superb affinity with whiskey, cognac, and especially Sambuca.

1¾ cup whole milk
¼ cup freshly roasted coffee beans in a medium
     grind
⅓ cup sugar, or to taste
6 egg yolks
2 tablespoons Kahlúa or another liqueur
1 teaspoon vanilla extract

Heat the milk and coffee in a medium saucepan over medium-low heat until it simmers. Turn off the heat, and let the mixture steep for 10 to 20 minutes or until it tastes strong enough for you. Strain the milk through a fine sieve lined with cheesecloth into a clean pot. Add the sugar and stir to dissolve, reheating the mixture, if necessary.

Beat the egg yolks until well combined, and add a little of the warm milk to the eggs, stirring constantly. This will temper the eggs, bringing the temperature up so they won't curdle when added to the pot. Add the tempered eggs to the pot, and cook, stirring all the while with a wooden spoon, over low heat, until the mixture thickens enough to coat the back the spoon. Never let the mixture come near boiling, or you will end up with scrambled eggs. The custard should not get hotter than 170°F. on a candy thermometer.

When the custard is ready, immediately remove it from the heat and strain it into a clean container to remove any lumps. Stir in the Kahlúa and the vanilla, and store, tightly covered, in the refrigerator for four or five days.

Makes 2½ cups

COFFEE-FLAVORED HONEY SAUCE

This wonderfully aromatic sauce is made by mixing coffee extract into melted honey, a suggestion given to me by my friend Joseph Steuer, a true epicurean. This sauce is particularly nice with poached or fresh fruit and with ice cream. It can also be used to glaze fruit and pastry. I find it very useful in dessert making of every kind. This sauce will keep for a very long time, properly stored. It is nice to have on hand to jazz up sliced peaches, or what have you. Sometimes I like to flavor this sauce with cinnamon or cardamom, depending on my mood.

You can use instant espresso if you cannot find coffee extract, but I find the flavor on the bitter side. Coffee extract is available by mail from Dean & Deluca, Maid of Scandinavia, and La Cuisine.

1 **cup mild honey, such as clover**
2 **tablespoons butter**
1 **teaspoon coffee extract or more**
Lemon juice to taste (optional)

Over medium heat in a small saucepan, melt the honey and the butter, and stir well to combine.

Stir in the coffee extract and taste the sauce. If it is too weak, add a few more drops of extract. To balance the flavors a little, add a squirt or two of lemon juice.

Use the sauce immediately while it is still warm, or refrigerate it in a tightly sealed jar until needed. Reheat sauce slowly over low heat or in the microwave.

Makes 1 cup

COFFEE SYRUP

This basic syrup can be used either as a sauce for desserts or as a flavoring for coffee drinks. It is perfect for sweetening iced coffee, and makes a splendid ice cream soda or Coffee Egg Cream (see page 72). For desserts, try adding spices to the boiling syrup for a different type of accent. Or use it as a liquid to poach fresh or dried fruit. Drizzle this syrup wherever you would drizzle anything sweet and liquid. It tastes just grand. You can double the recipe.

Vary this sauce, if you wish, by adding some cocoa to the syrup to make mocha syrup. Try adding 3 or 4 or more tablespoons of unsweetened cocoa to the syrup when you add the instant coffee. The cocoa adds richness and body to the sauce while remaining in the background. For a more pronounced chocolate taste, add even more cocoa, and maybe a drop or two of chocolate extract, which is available by mail from La Cuisine and Maid of Scandinavia.

1 cup sugar
½ cup water
3 teaspoons instant coffee or more

Over medium-high heat in a small saucepan, boil the sugar and water together until the sugar is dissolved and the mixture becomes thick and syrupy and coats the spoon.

Add the instant coffee and stir to combine. Cook the mixture for another minute or so, and then remove from heat. Store almost indefinitely in a clean jar with tight-fitting lid in the refrigerator.

Makes 1 cup

COFFEE-FLAVORED SABAYON SAUCE

This fluffy sauce is very simple to make and even easier to eat, as it just disappears on the tongue. I frequently use it to top peeled orange slices dusted with cinnamon. It makes a very refreshing winter dessert.

2 eggs
½ cup very strong brewed hot coffee
¼ cup sugar
Pinch of salt

In the top of a double boiler or in a small saucepan beat the eggs until combined. Add the coffee, beating well.

Place the pan over, but not touching, simmering water and beat in the sugar and salt. Continue beating until the sauce is frothy. Serve soon after making.

Makes 1 cup

MOCHA SAUCE

This velvet sauce is very dark and rich. Serve it on ice cream when hot fudge seems too rich. It is also perfect with profiteroles and many other pastries. An easy, versatile variation that you will find yourself using over and over.

4 ounces bittersweet chocolate, broken into pieces
2 tablespoons strong brewed coffee
4 tablespoons (½ stick) unsalted butter at room
temperature, in small pieces

In a saucepan or a double boiler, melt the chocolate over very low heat and stir well. Pour in the coffee and stir to combine. Remove from heat. Add the butter a little at a time, beating well. The sauce will thicken slightly and become glossy. Use immediately, or within a few hours.

Makes ¾ cup

ESPRESSO FUDGE SAUCE

A modern twist on an old-fashioned, sticky fudge sauce. Absolutely wonderful on everything, and even better by itself—from a spoon in the middle of the night.

There are many ways to jazz this sauce up. Try adding some liqueur, chopped nuts, or chopped pralines. Chopped candied orange and lemon peel are elegant additions as well.

6 tablespoons (¾ stick) unsalted butter
7 ounces bittersweet chocolate, chopped
¼ cup sugar
2 tablespoons instant espresso powder
⅔ cup heavy cream
1 teaspoon vanilla extract

In a medium saucepan, melt the butter.

Remove the pan from the heat and stir in the chocolate, sugar, espresso powder, and cream. Return to a medium flame and heat the mixture until it just boils, stirring constantly. Reduce the heat, and simmer the sauce until it is thick and sticky, 8 to 10 minutes. Remove it from heat and stir in the vanilla.

Use the sauce immediately, or refrigerate it in a jar with a tight-fitting lid for up to ten days. Seal the lid with plenty of masking tape to discourage midnight snackers.

Makes 1½ cups

CARAMEL COFFEE SAUCE

Luscious and sophisticated, this is simply a fabulous sauce, and probably my favorite, if I had to choose. Use cognac instead of the vanilla when you want a change, or add spices like ginger or nutmeg for something more exotic.

½ **cup water**
 1 **cup sugar**
 1 **cup strong brewed hot coffee**
½ **teaspoon lemon juice**
 1 **teaspoon vanilla extract**

In a medium saucepan combine the water and sugar and let sit until the sugar is moist.

Cook over medium heat, shaking the pan gently, until the sugar begins to caramelize and turn light brown.

Immediately remove the pan from the heat and carefully add the coffee. The sauce may boil and bubble up like a witches' brew, but do not be concerned—just stand back so you don't get burned.

Return the pan to a low flame and cook, stirring constantly, until all the caramel is dissolved. Remove from heat and let the sauce cool.

When the caramel is cool enough to touch, add the lemon juice and vanilla. Stir well and serve that day.

Makes 1 cup

CRÈME CHANTILLY AU CAFÉ

Basically this is a coffee-flavored, sweetened, lightly whipped cream. Serve it with granita di caffè for a cooling summer coffee break.

1 cup heavy cream, well chilled
1 teaspoon coffee extract
1 tablespoon liqueur (optional)
2 tablespoons sugar, or more to taste

In a metal bowl, combine the cream, the coffee extract, the liqueur if you are using it, and the sugar. Beat with an electric mixer or a wire whisk until the sugar dissolves. Taste the cream and add more sugar, if you wish.

Continue beating until soft peaks form. Serve soon after making, or refrigerate for up to two hours.

Makes 1½ cups

BUTTERSCOTCH SAUCE WITH COFFEE

This is perfect to pour over vanilla ice cream. There is nothing richer. Try sprinkling with toasted nuts for a textural contrast.

 1 cup brown sugar
 ¼ cup heavy cream
 ¼ cup (½ stick) unsalted butter
 Pinch of salt
 1 teaspoon coffee extract

In a medium-sized saucepan, mix together the brown sugar, cream, butter and salt. Cook over very low heat, stirring occasionally, until the sauce is thick and creamy, about 40 minutes.

Stir in the coffee extract and serve the sauce while it is still warm, or refrigerate it in a jar with a tight-fitting lid for one to two weeks. Gently reheat it over a low flame or in the microwave.

Makes 1 cup

COFFEE-COGNAC SAUCE

This simple, lush sauce gets better if it is made a few days in advance.

 1 cup heavy cream
 3 tablespoons medium-ground coffee beans
 ¼ cup sugar
 2 tablespoons cognac

In a small, heavy saucepan heat the cream until it just boils. Remove from the heat and add the ground coffee. Let the mixture steep for 20 minutes, and then strain it through a cheesecloth-lined sieve.

Add the sugar and stir until it dissolves, putting the sauce back on the heat if necessary. Stir in the cognac and refrigerate the sauce overnight.

Warm the sauce over low heat or in the microwave before serving.

Makes 1 cup

BREAKFAST RECIPES

FRUIT AND NUT BREAD

Perfect for toasting or for spreading with cream cheese. This waxy, compact loaf is replete with fruit and nuts and has a definite coffee flavor. It has been a favorite of mine for years.

½ cup coarsely chopped dates
½ cup coarsely chopped prunes
½ cup coarsely chopped apricots
½ cup golden raisins
1 cup boiling water
1 cup strong brewed hot coffee
2 eggs
¾ cups brown sugar
1 teaspoon vanilla extract
1 cup all-purpose flour
1½ cups whole wheat flour
2 teaspoons baking powder
1 teaspoon baking soda
½ cup bran
1 cup coarsely chopped walnuts

Heat the oven to 350°F. Grease and flour a metal loaf pan. (If you must use a glass pan, set the oven temperature at 325°F.)

Combine the dried fruits with the boiling water and the hot coffee, and set aside.

Beat the eggs with the brown sugar until they are well combined and thick, about 1 minute. Stir in the vanilla.

Sift together the flours, baking powder, and soda.

Add half of the flour mixture to the egg mixture and stir to combine. Then add all of the dried fruit mixture and the rest of the flour mixture, mixing well after each addition. Mix in the bran and the walnuts and stir until just combined.

Scrape the batter into the prepared loaf pan and bake for about 1 hour or until the loaf is crusty and brown and a tester inserted into the center comes out clean and dry.

Cool the bread in the pan on a rack for 10 minutes; then unmold and finish cooling. Wrap tightly and refrigerate, preferably overnight.

IRISH COFFEE MUFFINS

These are terrific little treats: moist, decadent, and dense. For a chocolaty version, add some chocolate chips to the batter before baking.

¾ **cup all-purpose flour**
½ **teaspoon baking soda**
¼ **teaspoon salt**
½ **cup (1 stick) butter at room temperature**
½ **cup sugar**
1 **egg**
1 **tablespoon instant coffee granules**
2 **tablespoons Irish whiskey**
½ **cup chocolate chips (optional)**

Heat the oven to 400°F. Grease the cups of a regular-size muffin pan.

Sift together the flour, baking soda, and salt.

In a large bowl, beat the butter with the sugar until fluffy, about 1 minute. Add the egg, and beat well.

Dissolve the coffee granules in the whiskey and add this mixture to the butter mixture. Beat well. Gently mix in the dry ingredients until just incorporated. Do not overmix. Fold in the chocolate chips if you are using them.

Spoon the batter into the muffin tins and bake for 18 to 20 minutes, or until a cake tester inserted into the center of one of the center muffins comes out clean.

Cool the muffins in the tin on a rack for ten minutes. Unmold them and let them cool completely. Serve them warm, or reheat them before serving. They also freeze well. To defrost, wrap them in foil and heat in a 300°F. oven for 15 minutes or until they are warm throughout.

Makes 12 muffins

GINGERED ESPRESSO SCHNECKEN

Rich, moist, and gooey, the sweetness of these luscious buns is tempered by the brightness of the coffee and the zing of the ginger. They are best baked the same day you plan to serve them, but you can make the dough and filling in advance and just leave the assembly and final rising for the last minute. Beware, even the most polite houseguest has been known to devour these buns ravenously.

For the Dough:
   1 **package yeast**
   1 **cup warm (110°F.) whole milk**
4–5 **cups all-purpose flour**
   ½ **cup (1 stick) unsalted butter at room temperature**
   ½ **cup granulated sugar**
   2 **eggs**
   ½ **teaspoon salt**
   1 **teaspoon ground ginger**
   1 **tablespoon finely grated lemon zest**

For the Filling:
   ¼ **cup very finely chopped candied ginger**
   ¼ **cup granulated sugar**
   ½ **cup melted butter**
   2 **teaspoons instant espresso (powdered or granular)**
   ¼ **cup mild honey**
   ½ **cup brown sugar**

Generously butter 18 muffin cups.

Dissolve the yeast in the warm milk and let sit for a few minutes. Mix in 2 cups of the flour and reserve.

Cream the butter with the ½ cup granulated sugar until light and fluffy. Mix in the eggs, beating well after each addition. Beat in the salt, ground ginger, and lemon zest. Alternately beat in half of the yeast mixture with half of the remaining flour, beating well after each addition. Repeat until both are used up. Knead the dough until it is smooth and elastic, about 10 minutes by hand and 5 with a machine. Form dough into a ball and lightly butter it all around. Place dough in a deep bowl and cover with plastic wrap. Let dough rise in a warm place until it has doubled in bulk, about 1½ hours. A quick way to raise the dough is to warm the oven to 200°F., place the bowl of dough in the oven, and turn off the heat. It will double in bulk in 45–60 minutes. You can also raise the dough in the refrigerator overnight and just proceed where you left off.

When the dough is doubled in bulk, punch it down and knead it for a minute. Roll it into a rectangle ¼ inch thick. Sprinkle with the candied ginger and the ¼ cup granulated sugar. Roll the dough up tightly as if for a jelly roll, and cut it into 18 slices.

Mix together the melted butter, instant espresso, honey, and brown sugar. Divide this mixture evenly among the buttered muffin tins. Press the sliced rolls, cut side down, into the muffin cups. Cover the dough and let it rise for 45 to 60 minutes in a warm spot, until doubled in bulk.

Uncover the schnecken. Heat the oven to 400°F. and bake the schnecken for 15 minutes. Reduce the oven temperature to 325°F. and bake an additional 7 to 10 minutes, or until golden brown. Remove from the oven and let the schnecken cool for a minute or so. Then invert them onto a platter and serve immediately or within the hour.

Makes 18 schnecken

ORANGE WAFFLES WITH ESPRESSO BUTTER

The idea for this recipe made me schlep home my parents' ancient waffle iron. It was worth the haul, because the combination of zesty orange waffles coated with meltingly rich coffee butter was truly special. Don't limit yourself to serving these beauties for breakfast and brunch. I actually prefer them for dinner, but then, I like soup and salad for breakfast, too.

The cake flour makes the waffles extra tender, and separating the eggs makes them extra light.

For the Waffles:
  2 cups cake flour
  3 teaspoons baking powder
½ teaspoon salt
  3 egg yolks
¾ cup whole milk
¼ cup orange juice
  2 tablespoons finely grated orange zest
¾ cup half-and-half
¼ cup melted butter
  3 egg whites
  3 tablespoons granulated sugar

For the Espresso Butter:
½ cup (1 stick) unsalted butter at room temperature
  2 tablespoons confectioner's sugar
  1 tablespoon instant espresso (powdered or granular)
  2 teaspoons hot water

Sift together the cake flour, baking powder, and salt.

In a separate bowl, beat the egg yolks, milk, orange juice, orange zest, half-and-half, and melted butter until they are well combined and thick, about 1 minute. Fold in the flour mixture and mix until just smooth.

Beat the egg whites until they are foamy, and add the granulated sugar. Continue beating until the whites hold stiff peaks when the beaters are slowly raised.

Gently fold about one-third of the egg whites into the batter to lighten it. Then fold in the remaining whites until just incorporated. Be careful not to overbeat and deflate the whites.

Bake the waffles in a waffle iron according to manufacturer's instructions.

While the waffles are baking, make the coffee butter. In an electric mixer combine the butter and confectioner's sugar and beat until smooth and fluffy, about 1 minute. Dissolve the instant espresso in the hot water and beat this into the butter until combined. Pack the espresso butter into a decorative crock or a small bowl and refrigerate until serving time.

Serve the waffles while they are still warm with the espresso butter. You may want to have some extra confectioner's sugar on hand.

Makes 6 waffles

Note: If your waffle iron is like mine, a relic from another era with the instructions long lost, here are some tips. Plug the iron in and heat it for a minute or two. Grease it lightly with butter (don't forget to grease the upper half) and when the foam starts to subside, the iron is hot enough for your batter. Pour in about ½ cup of batter and close the lid. Bake until golden brown. Transfer waffle to a plate and keep it warm while you make the rest. If your waffle sticks, bake it for a few seconds longer. If it still sticks, use the tip of a small sharp knife to loosen it. If it still sticks, well, then you are in trouble. Rip the waffle out and begin again. Use more butter this time.

CAPPUCCINO PANCAKES

The most requested breakfast in my home is this spicy delight: creamy cinnamon pancakes glazed with coffee syrup. Try adding blueberries, banana slices, pecans, or chocolate chips to the batter as well. They are all delicious variations.

¾ **cup half-and-half**
2 **tablespoons melted butter**
1 **egg**
1 **cup flour**
2 **teaspoons baking powder**
2 **tablespoons sugar**
½ **teaspoon salt**
1 **teaspoon cinnamon**
Butter
1 **cup Coffee Syrup (see page 189)**

In a large bowl, whisk together the half-and-half, the melted butter, and the egg.

In a separate bowl, sift together the flour, baking powder, sugar, salt, and cinnamon. Add this to the egg mixture and stir until just combined.

Place a griddle or large frying pan over medium-high heat and butter it lightly. Heat the pan until a drop of water bounces and skids off the surface. Pour some batter onto the griddle and cook it until bubbles cover the top and the underside is browned. Flip the cake over and brown the other side.

Transfer the pancakes to a serving plate and keep them warm. Continue until all of the batter is used up, buttering the pan as necessary.

Serve the pancakes at once with butter and Coffee Syrup.

Serves 4–6

APPETIZERS

WARM LENTIL SALAD WITH WALNUTS

Since coffee has some of the same qualities as smoky, earthy bacon, I like to use it as a flavorful and light alternative. I served this dish as a main course to some vegetarian friends who were enraptured by the richness of the lentils paired with the brightness of the green garnish. Serve this salad with some chewy bread and a bit of tangy cheese, and your guests will adore it, vegetarians or not.

Lentilles de Puy, are tiny greenish disks from France which cook much faster than the brown ones, maintaining their plump little shape without falling to mush. You can buy these lentils at gourmets markets, or order them from Dean & Deluca or La Cuisine. If you cannot get them, use the regular kind, but be careful when you mix them up with the vinaigrette, or they are likely to fall apart.

The lentil mixture is best prepared the day before so the flavors have a chance to mature.

For the Lentils:
 1 cup lentilles de Puy, picked over and rinsed
 ½ cup strong brewed coffee
 1 bay leaf
 1 small onion, peeled and thickly sliced
 1 quart water

For the Vinaigrette:
 1 teaspoon Dijon-style mustard
 ¾ teaspoon salt
 2 tablespoons red wine vinegar
 ½ cup walnut oil
Freshly ground pepper

For the Garnish:
 1 tablespoon olive oil
 1 cup walnut halves
 2 garlic cloves, minced
 3 tablespoons minced fresh chives
Salt and pepper
 8 cups mixed greens, such as arugula, watercress,
        Boston lettuce, chicory, radicchio, beet greens,
        etc., washed and dried
Whole chives, with their purple flowers

In a large saucepan, combine the lentils, coffee, bay leaf, and onion, and water. Bring the water to a boil, and simmer the lentils, skimming occasionally, for 20 to 30 minutes, or until they are tender. Cooking time will vary greatly due to the age of the lentils.

While the lentils are simmering, make the vinaigrette by whisking together all of the ingredients until the sauce is thick and smooth. Taste and correct seasonings.

When lentils are tender, drain them, discard the bay leaf and onion, and combine the lentils with half of the vinaigrette. Mix carefully but thoroughly until all the lentils are coated. Cover the mixture and refrigerate for several hours or overnight.

An hour before serving, bring lentils to room temperature.

Just before serving, heat the olive oil in a skillet until hot but not smoking. Add the walnuts and sauté them over medium-low heat until they begin to turn golden and release their scent. Add the garlic and sauté for another minute until the garlic turns opaque; do not let the garlic brown. Add the walnut mixture and chives to the lentils and mix well. Season to taste with salt and pepper.

Toss the salad greens with the remaining vinaigrette and divide among 6 to 8 salad plates. Top with the lentils and garnish with the whole chives. Serve immediately while the lentils are still warm from the walnuts.

Serves 6–8

Variations: Fry some day-old bread cubes with the walnuts, adding extra garlic and olive oil as necessary, until they are golden brown. Instead of mixing the walnuts directly into the lentils, place them with the croutons on top as garnish. I love to serve this version as a light entrée, or as part of a luncheon buffet.

You could also substitute small cubes of blanched lardons (French bacon) for the bread. This results in a lusty main course for a cool winter evening. Serve something light for dessert, like Poached Pears (page 171) or Orange Salad (page 174) for a properly balanced meal.

WHITE BEAN PESTO WITH COFFEE AND ROSEMARY

Coffee and beans are a terrific combination, and this time I have paired them in an Italian-inspired bean paste. If you mash the beans down, you will have a thick dip perfect for stuffing into cherry tomatoes or slathering on thin slices of toasted sourdough.

Left whole, the beans make a wonderful salad to be eaten alone, as part of an antipasto plate, or with grilled shrimp and scallops. This is a versatile, very simple dish that I seem to make over and over, much to the delight of my friends and family.

If it is at all possible, cook the beans yourself. The texture is far superior to that of the canned variety. An easy way to do this is to bring picked-over beans to a boil on the stove, and then bake them, covered, at 250°F. for 1½ hours. You will not have to be attentive to them at all during this time, and the rewards are great for such a meager bit of effort. Cooked beans freeze excellently.

3 tablespoons olive oil, divided
2 garlic cloves, minced
3 tablespoons strong brewed coffee
2 cups cooked or canned white beans, well rinsed
3 tablespoons fresh rosemary leaves, or 1 tablespoon
        dried
Salt and pepper

In a heavy, preferably nonstick, skillet, heat 1 tablespoon of the olive oil until hot but not smoking. Add the garlic and sauté for one minute until the garlic releases its scent and turns opaque. Stir in the coffee and simmer the mixture for 30 seconds over medium heat.

Add the beans and cook them until they absorb the coffee, about 1 minute. If the beans seem too dry, add a bit of water. Stir in the rosemary, the remaining olive oil, and salt and pepper to taste, and remove from heat.

Let the mixture cool to room temperature. Serve immediately or refrigerate, covered, for up to five days. If you want to use these beans for a dip, do not mash them until close to serving time. Add a bit of olive oil, if necessary, to smooth the texture. It is nice, although not imperative, to leave the puree a bit chunky.

Makes 2 cups

PÂTÉ AU CAFÉ

Coffee and Madeira wine heighten and intensify the smooth, flavor of chicken livers. This fragrant golden paste studded with raisins and bacon is splendid served with crackers and cocktails.

Make this the day before you want to serve it.

¼ **pound bacon, cut into small pieces**
 1 **pound chicken livers**
¼ **cup brewed coffee**
¼ **cup Madeira**
¾ **cup heavy cream**
 1 **cup chopped yellow onion**
¼ **cup mayonnaise**
 1 **tablespoon Dijon-style mustard**
 1 **teaspoon herbs de Provence**
¼ **teaspoon freshly ground nutmeg**
Salt and pepper
½ **cup golden raisins**
 3 **tablespoons finely chopped Italian parsley**

Fry the bacon until crisp and drain on paper towels, reserving the fat.

Over a medium flame, sauté the chicken livers in the bacon fat until they are golden brown on the outside but still pink in the middle. Lift the liver out of the pan with a slotted spoon and reserve.

Over high heat, deglaze the pan with the coffee and Madeira, scraping up all the browned bits. Pour in the cream and let it boil for 1 minute. Remove from heat.

In a food processor, combine the chicken livers, onion, mayonnaise, mustard, herbs de Provence, and nutmeg, and process until they are blended. Pour in the cream mixture and process until the mixture is smooth. Season with salt and pepper to taste.

Add the golden raisins, parsley, and the reserved bacon and process just to combine the ingredients without pulverizing them. Spoon the pâté into a decorative serving bowl or crock, and cover the top with plastic wrap. Refrigerate overnight, or for up to four days. Let the pâté come to room temperature before serving.

Makes about 3 cups

SKEWERED COFFEE SHRIMP WITH GARLIC AND MUSHROOMS

This lovely, colorful hors d'oeuvre never fails to delight the sophisticated finger-food crowd. You can use other vegetables besides mushrooms; red and green peppers are tasty, as are thick slices of zucchini and cubes of eggplant. Be creative; this dish takes well to change. Scallops make a nice substitute for the shrimp, but they cook faster, so watch them carefully.

  4 **tablespoons melted butter**
  4 **tablespoons olive oil**
  2 **garlic cloves, minced**
  1 **teaspoon dried thyme**
⅛ **teaspoon cayenne**
¼ **teaspoon cumin**
1½ **teaspoons salt**
Juice of 1 lemon
  2 **tablespoon strong brewed coffee**
  2 **pounds medium shrimp, shelled**
  1 **pound white cultivated mushrooms, trimmed and cleaned**
  1 **French baguette, cut into 2-inch diagonal slices**

Heat the broiler.

In a small bowl, whisk together the butter, olive oil, garlic, thyme, cayenne, cumin, salt, lemon juice, and coffee until well combined.

On each of 12 to 16 hors d'oeuvre skewers, thread one shrimp, then a mushroom, then another shrimp. Lay each completed skewer on a broiler pan as you go.

Pour the butter mixture evenly over the skewers. Broil them under a high flame for about 3 minutes on each side, or until the shrimp have turned pink and the garlic is opaque.

Remove the pan from the broiler and cap each skewer with a slice of bread. Serve immediately.

Serves 12 to 16

SOUP

COUNTERFEIT PASSOVER RUSSEL

Russel is a traditional Russian Jewish soup served at Passover over hard-boiled eggs (for non-Russian Jews, the eggs are covered in salted water). The egg symbolizes new life and hope, while the sour russel and salty water symbolize the hardships and tears of the Jewish people. In my family, we served both russel and salt water and let people choose which to pour over their egg.

Usually we depended on my great-aunt Martha to either make russel (which is made from fermented beets and is similar to a sour-flavored borscht) or to buy it from one of the Russian stores in Coney Island. However, when Aunt Martha moved from Brooklyn to Florida, nobody else thought to buy the russel that year.

My father remembered the evening of the seder just before the guests arrived, and knew what kind of moaning he would have to endure for having forgotten the russel. In our family, with the relocation of so many relatives to faraway places, and the death of so many others, we rely heavily on tradition to keep the rest of us together. Russel was more than just soup, and its absence would intensify the feelings of yet another loss.

Rather than face this, my father came up with a brilliant idea: he would make counterfeit russel using a mixture of borscht and souring agents. For these he chose red wine vinegar and coffee, in varying amounts. The result was so delightful that we never went back to real russel again. Of course we never told the rest of the family our little secret.

I guess they all know now.

1 quart prepared borscht (Mother's or Manischewitz)
1 cup brewed coffee
Red wine vinegar
Salt and pepper
½ cup chopped fresh dill
6 hard-boiled eggs

Heat the borscht slowly in a large pot over low heat. Add the coffee and stir to combine.

Start with 1 tablespoon of red wine vinegar, and keep adding more, tablespoon at a time, until the borscht is sour but not mouth-puckering.

Season the soup with salt and pepper to taste and add the dill. Place one hard-boiled egg in each of six serving bowls and pour some of the "russel" over it. Serve immediately.

Serves 6

COLD CURRIED TOMATO SOUP WITH COFFEE

This is the perfect summer luncheon dish. When its too hot to eat anything else, this will slide right down leaving a tasty, spicy trail on your tongue. And it's a snap to make. I like to garnish this soup with lots of fresh cilantro, but any other fresh herb will work well. Make sure that your curry powder is fresh and flavorful, or the soup may acquire the cupboardlike flavor of stale curry. The sugar is only necessary if you think the acidity of the tomatoes needs balancing out. Taste it first. Use an acidic coffee such as Margogipe or a true mocha for this soup.

  1 tablespoon butter or olive oil
  2 teaspoons curry powder
  2 tablespoons tomato paste
  1 cup strong brewed coffee
  6 cups tomato juice
  2 tomatoes, seeded and chopped
  8 scallions, minced
  ½ teaspoon ground ginger
Juice of 1 lemon
Grated zest of 1 lemon
Dash of Tabasco sauce
Salt and pepper
  1 teaspoon sugar (optional)
  1 cup sour cream (optional)
  1 cup chopped fresh cilantro

In a small skillet over a medium flame heat the butter or oil until hot. Add the curry powder and sauté it for about 30 seconds to take the raw edge off of the curry.

Add the tomato paste and the coffee, and stir well to

combine. Simmer the mixture for about 1 minute until the tomato paste is dissolved. Remove from heat.

In a large bowl, mix together all the other ingredients except the sour cream and cilantro. Refrigerate the soup, covered, for at least 3 hours, and up to two days.

When ready to serve, ladle the soup into serving bowls and garnish each bowl with 1 tablespoon of the sour cream and some of the cilantro. Place the remaining sour cream on the table and let people help themselves.

Serves 6–8

HEARTY ONION COFFEE SOUP

This hearty soup overflows with pasta, tiny green peas, and thick slices of onion. It is a meal in itself, but is also perfect to serve before a fish or vegetable entrée. It freezes well, so feel free to double the recipe.

If you cannot find fresh peas, use frozen ones. Just make sure they are petits pois and not the large ones.

2 tablespoons olive oil
4 or 5 large, sweet Spanish onions, sliced
3 garlic cloves, minced
1 bay leaf
½ teaspoon dried oregano
1 teaspoon dried thyme
1 large bunch fresh parsley, chopped
1 cup shelled fresh petits pois (tiny green peas)
2 cups brewed coffee
4 cups beef broth
½ cup tiny pasta (orzo, tubettini, or pastina)
Salt and pepper
1 cup chopped fresh parsley or basil
1 cup freshly grated Parmesan cheese (optional)

In a large kettle over a medium flame heat the olive oil until it is hot but not smoking. Add the onions and sauté for 10 minutes, stirring occasionally, until they begin to brown. Add the garlic, bay leaf, oregano, thyme, and parsley, and turn the heat to low. Partially cover the pot and let the mixture simmer for another 20 to 30 minutes, or until the onions are soft. Stir the mixture from time to time so everything gets evenly cooked.

Add the peas, coffee, and beef broth to the pot and turn the heat up so the mixture comes to a boil. Then reduce the heat and partially cover the pot. Let the soup simmer for another 35 minutes.

Stir in the pasta and add salt and pepper to taste. Let the soup simmer until the pasta is soft (check the package for timing).

Ladle the soup into bowls and garnish with the additional parsley or basil, and Parmesan cheese if you wish. Serve immediately.

Serves 6–8

CREAM OF MUSHROOM SOUP

This rich soup is best served in small quantities. It is really an excellent use of coffee in a soup, as the coffee's distinct flavor permeates and enlivens the other ingredients.

For a lower fat version of this soup, substitute skim milk for the whole milk and nonfat yogurt for the sour cream.

 2 tablespoons olive oil
 3 large onions, chopped
 1 pound fresh mushrooms, cleaned and sliced
 1 small garlic clove, minced
 1 cup brewed coffee
 1 tablespoon paprika
Dash of Tabasco sauce
 3 tablespoons butter
 4 tablespoons flour
 1 cup milk
2½ cups chicken stock
Salt and pepper
 1 tablespoon lemon juice (optional)
¼ cup chopped fresh dill
¾ cup sour cream
Fresh dill sprigs

In a medium-sized saucepan over a medium flame, heat the olive oil until hot but not smoking. Add the onions and sauté them for about 10 minutes, stirring occasionally, until they start to wilt. Add the mushrooms and garlic, and sauté for another minute until the garlic turns opaque but not brown. Add the coffee, paprika, and Tabasco sauce and lower the heat. Cover the pan and let the mixture simmer for 15 more minutes.

While the mixture is simmering, make a roux. In a large saucepan or medium-sized pot melt the butter over medium heat. Whisk in the flour and cook, whisking constantly, for 4 to 5 minutes. Add the milk and cook, whisking frequently, for about 10 minutes or until the mixture thickens.

Add the mushroom mixture to the milk and mix well. Stir in the stock and season with salt and pepper to taste. Simmer the mixture for another 15 minutes.

Taste the soup and add the lemon juice if you think it needs it. Stir in the chopped dill and sour cream until well combined, and serve immediately, garnished with the dill sprigs.

Serves 6

AUTUMN VEGETABLE PEANUT SOUP WITH COFFEE

This luscious soup is the perfect first course for Thanksgiving dinner. Made with two seasonal favorites, squash and sweet potatoes, it is further enhanced by the additions of peanuts, ginger, and coffee. It is a simply stunning soup.

To prepare the squash puree you can either bake two acorn squashes, split in half and seeded, in a 375°F oven for 1 hour and then puree their flesh in a food processor, or you can use frozen squash puree. The baking adds richness to the squashes' flavor, but the frozen packages are a major time-saver. Use your judgment.

1 **cup roasted unsalted peanuts**
2 **tablespoons butter**
1 **small onion, minced**
1 **small garlic clove, minced**
2 **tablespoons grated fresh ginger**
1 **teaspoon dried thyme**
4 **cups pureed cooked winter squash**
2 **cups pureed cooked sweet potatoes**
1 **cup brewed coffee**
5 **cups chicken stock**

Salt and pepper
1 cup minced fresh chives or parsley

In a food processor, puree the peanuts until they become peanut butter. Set aside.

Melt the butter in a soup pot over medium heat. Add the onion and sauté for about 10 minutes or until it is wilted. Add the garlic, ginger, and thyme, and sauté for another few minutes, stirring constantly so the garlic doesn't burn.

Remove the mixture from the heat and puree it in the food processor with the peanuts. Pulse on and off until the mixture is smooth.

Return the onion and peanut butter mixture to the kettle and stir in the squash, potatoes, coffee, and chicken stock. Season to taste with salt and pepper. Simmer the soup for 20 minutes and adjust seasonings, if necessary.

Ladle the soup into bowls, garnish with the chives or parsley, and serve immediately.

Serves 8–10

RED BEAN AND HAM SOUP

This is one of my favorite soups, which I serve at a variety of occasions. I like to double the recipe and freeze individual portions in yogurt containers. Just remember to label them, or you might end up as I once did: defrosting hot fudge to find black bean soup instead. Not very appealing to spoon over ice cream, that's for certain.

Make sure to use freshly cooked or frozen kidney beans for this recipe; the canned ones disintegrate into mush.

3 tablespoons olive oil
1 large yellow onion, chopped
1 cup diced celery
2 garlic cloves, minced
2 cups cooked red kidney beans
1 bay leaf
¼ cup chopped fresh parsley
1 ham hock
Dash of Tabasco sauce
2 cups brewed coffee
Salt and pepper

In a large kettle, heat the olive oil over a medium flame until it is hot but not smoking. Add the onion and celery, and sauté the mixture for 10 minutes, stirring frequently. Add the garlic and sauté for another minute until the garlic turns opaque.

Add the kidney beans, bay leaf, parsley, ham hock, Tabasco sauce, and coffee, and stir to combine. Then add enough water to cover the ingredients in the pot by 2 inches.

Bring the soup to a boil, and then lower the heat. Simmer the soup for about 50 minutes. Taste and season with the salt and pepper to taste. Remove from heat.

Cool the soup for about 20 minutes. With a slotted spoon, remove half of the beans and puree them in a food processor. Return them to the pot.

Remove the ham hock and dice the meat into small pieces. Mix the meat into the soup and discard the bone. Serve the soup at once, or refrigerate it in well-sealed containers for up to five days.

To serve refrigerated soup, gently reheat it. If it is too thick, thin it with hot water or chicken stock. Correct the seasonings and serve immediately.

Serves 6–8

FRUITS OF THE EARTH SOUP

This soup combines different fruits of the earth (vegetables that grow underground) with earthy-flavored coffee. It is elegant and homey at once and can be served at a variety of occasions. It is a filling soup that tastes terrific in the winter when some food begins to lose its flavor. Have a bowl of this and your tired taste buds will rejoice.

- 2 **tablespoons olive oil**
- 1 **tablespoon butter**
- 2 **large yellow onions, chopped**
- 2 **garlic cloves, minced**
- 1 **cup diced carrots**
- 1 **cup diced fennel**
- 1 **teaspoon celery seeds**
- ½ **teaspoon dried tarragon**
- 1 **parsnip, peeled and diced**
- 1 **turnip, diced**
- 4 **potatoes, diced**
- 1 **cup brewed coffee**
- 3 **cups chicken stock**

Salt and pepper

- 1 **bunch watercress, rinsed and minced**
- ½ **cup light cream or half-and-half**
- 1½ **cups croutons, preferably homemade**

In a large kettle over a medium flame, heat the olive oil and butter until the butter melts. Add the onions, garlic, carrots, and fennel and gently sauté the vegetables until they begin to soften and wilt, about 15 minutes. Stir frequently.

Add the celery seeds, tarragon, parsnip, turnip, potatoes,

coffee, and stock. Season with salt and pepper to taste, and simmer the soup until the vegetables are tender but not mushy, about 30 minutes. Add the watercress and simmer for 2 more minutes.

Let the soup cool for about 15 minutes. Puree half of the soup in a food processor and return it to the pot.

Add the cream to the kettle and reheat the soup over a low flame, stirring constantly. Serve the hot soup immediately garnished with croutons.

Serves 6–8

COFFEE CHEESE SOUP

This recipe combines sharp and spicy coffee with rich, succulent Brie and tangy Parmesan cheese for a creamy soup that will warm your soul during winter's chill. Perfect for those Sunday nights at home with a fire, a book, a glass of wine, and watercress salad.

  4 tablespoons butter
  4 tablespoons all-purpose flour
  1 cup milk
  1 cup brewed coffee
  2 cups chicken stock
  1 teaspoon prepared mustard
  2 cups diced Brie cheese
½ cup freshly grated Parmesan cheese
Dash of Tabasco sauce
Salt and pepper
  6 slices whole wheat toast
⅔ cup minced fresh chives, or ⅓ cup minced scallions
      combined with ⅓ cup minced parsley

In a medium-sized saucepan, melt the butter over low heat. Add the flour and cook the mixture for several minutes, stirring often. Add the milk and stir constantly until the mixture thickens, about 7 minutes.

Add the coffee, chicken stock, and mustard, and gently heat the mixture through. Add the cheeses and stir until they just melt. Remove the pan from the heat, stir in the Tabasco sauce, and season with salt and pepper to taste.

In each of six bowls, place one slice of toast. Ladle the soup over the bread and garnish with the chives or scallions and parsley. Serve immediately.

Serves 6

MAIN COURSES

LAMB STEW WITH VEGETABLES AND COFFEE

This exotic stew offers just the right balance between rich lamb chunks and colorful vegetables. I like to serve it in the dead of winter when its lovely colors brighten gray days. It is a good idea to make this the day before you plan to serve it so the flavors have a chance to blend. Just reheat it in a 350°F. oven for 40 minutes or until it's heated through. It also freezes well.

1 cup strong brewed coffee
Finely grated zest of 1 lemon
Juice of 1 lemon
 1 small yellow onion, chopped
 2 garlic cloves, minced
 ¼ cup chopped fresh basil
 4 tablespoons olive oil
 1 teaspoon dried rosemary
 1 teaspoon dried thyme
Freshly ground pepper
 2 pound boneless lamb shoulder, cut into cubes
 2 tablespoons all-purpose flour

1½ cups dry white wine
1½ cups beef broth
  3 tablespoons tomato paste
  1 cup sliced carrots
  1 cup sliced parsnips
  2 cups cooked chick-peas, white beans, or lima
      beans
  1 cup sliced zucchini
Salt and pepper (optional)
  ½ cup minced fresh parsley

In a large bowl, make a marinade by combining the coffee, lemon zest, lemon juice, onion, garlic, basil, 2 tablespoons of the olive oil, rosemary, thyme, and pepper. Mix
well to combine.

Add the lamb chunks, turning to coat with marinade, and
cover the bowl with plastic wrap. Let the lamb marinate
for 2 to 3 hours at room temperature, or overnight in the
refrigerator. (You can freeze the lamb in the marinade for
up to 3 months.)

Heat the oven to 350°F. Remove the lamb from the marinade and brush off any onion or basil that cling to the
chunks. Dry the meat on paper towels. Reserve the marinade.

Heat the remaining 2 tablespoons olive oil over a medium flame in a large pot, and brown the lamb on all sides,
working in small batches. Transfer the browned lamb to
papers towels to drain.

When all the lamb is browned, discard the olive oil and
wipe the pot clean.

Return the lamb to the pot and sprinkle the flour over it.
Cook the lamb for a few minutes over medium heat until
the flour turns golden brown. Stir constantly.

Stir in the marinade, wine, broth, tomato paste, carrots,

and parsnips. Cover the pot and bake it in the oven for 45 minutes.

Add the beans and zucchini to the stew and bake for another 25 minutes, uncovered. The vegetables should be cooked through but not mushy. If you like mushy vegetables, continue to bake the stew until they are cooked enough for your taste.

Remove the stew from the oven, stir well to evenly distribute the lamb and vegetables, and taste. Season with salt and pepper if necessary. Garnish with the parsley and serve immediately.

Serves 6–8

RISOTTO WITH CABBAGE AND SAUSAGE

Substituting coffee for part of the stock to make risotto was my mother's idea. She is the family risotto expert and loves to experiment with different combinations. She originally suggested using coffee with a mushroom risotto, but I happened to have a lovely head of cabbage in my refrigerator when I was ready for testing. Do try substituting sautéed mushrooms for the cabbage, I'm certain the risotto will be delicious!

I used dill in this recipe. While it is not commonly used in Italian cooking, it goes nicely with the cabbage. Substitute another herb if you prefer.

You must use Arborio rice (short-grained Italian rice) to make risotto; any other type of rice will disintegrate. It is available in many fine supermarkets, and by mail from Dean & Deluca and Williams-Sonoma.

Make sure that the broth is still simmering when you add it to the rice, or the risotto will not work. You can prepare this dish in a heavy saucepan, if you wish, but the risotto will cook faster in a skillet because the rice will have more surface area near the heat to help it absorb the liquid.

2 tablespoons olive oil
2 tablespoons butter
1 medium yellow onion, chopped
2 links hot or sweet Italian sausage, sliced
1 garlic clove, minced
1 small head of cabbage, trimmed and shredded
¼ cup chopped fresh dill
2 cup Arborio rice
½ cup strong freshly brewed hot coffee
6 cups chicken broth, brought to a simmer and
        kept hot
Salt and pepper
½ cup freshly grated Parmesan cheese

Over low heat, melt the olive oil and butter in a large, heavy saucepan or skillet. Add the onion and sauté it until it begins to wilt, about 3 minutes.

Add the sausage and the garlic and sauté until the garlic releases its aroma and turns opaque. Stir frequently.

Add the cabbage and dill and sauté the mixture until the cabbage softens and wilts, about 7 minutes.

Add the rice and stir to coat all the grains with the olive oil and butter. Add the coffee and stir gently. Simmer until the coffee is absorbed.

Add ½ cup of the hot broth to the risotto, stirring frequently. As the rice absorbs the hot broth, add another ½ cup, and continue until all the broth is incorporated into the rice. This is a slow process, but it is worth it, so be patient; adding more broth before the last batch is absorbed will lead to watery risotto.

When all the broth is gone, add salt and pepper to taste and stir in the Parmesan cheese. Serve immediately. Risotto will not wait.

Serves 6

CURRIED CHICKEN BREASTS WITH FIGS

A spicy-sweet combination in which the smoki-ness of the coffee endows the meaty figs with a new dimension. This is an elegant dinner party dish that is also easy enough to serve every day. You can serve it with buttered rice or noodles, or maybe with a nut-ted barley pilaf, if you want to really impress.

Make sure to use flavorful curry powder or your dish will taste flat. If you prefer a spicy mix, leave a few of the seeds of the jalapeño chile pepper attached to the flesh; the seeds hold the fire of any chile.

½ **cup chopped dried figs**
1 **cup freshly brewed strong hot coffee**
3 **tablespoons olive oil**
6 **boned and skinned chicken breasts**
1 **tablespoon butter**
1 **small onion, chopped**
2 **garlic cloves, minced**
½ **small jalapeño chile pepper, seeded and chopped**
1 **small Granny Smith or other tart cooking apple,**
    peeled, cored, and chopped
2 **tablespoons flour**

1½ **tablespoons curry powder**
 ½ **teaspoon cardamom seeds, bruised with a pestle
      or the side of a heavy knife**
 1 **teaspoon coriander powder**
 1 **teaspoon salt, or to taste**
 2 **cups chicken broth**
Grated zest of 1 lime
Juice of 1 lime

In a small bowl, combine the figs with the hot coffee and reserve.

In a large skillet, heat 2 tablespoons of the olive oil over medium-high heat. Brown the chicken breasts on both sides and keep them warm.

Melt the butter and the remaining 1 tablespoon olive oil in the skillet and then add the onion. Sauté for 5 minutes, or until the onion begins to soften. Add the garlic, jalapeño, and apple and sauté for another 2 minutes, stirring constantly.

Add the flour, curry powder, bruised cardamom seeds, coriander powder, and salt. Stir well and cook for 2 more minutes. Add the chicken broth, lime zest and juice. Stir in reserved figs and coffee, and boil the sauce for 1 or 2 minutes, stirring constantly, until it thickens slightly.

Add the chicken and sauté it for a minute or two, or until the breasts are cooked through. Serve immediately.

Serves 6

STEAK AU POIVRE ET CAFÉ

This wonderful classic is further enhanced by the addition of coffee to the sauce. If you prefer not to use the cognac in the recipe, leave it out and use more coffee instead, although it will not ignite. You can crack the peppercorns with a mortar and pestle, hammer, meat pounder, or the side of a knife.

Serve these steaks with french fries or another starch to soak up the wonderful sauce.

1 large shell steak (New York strip steak), about 1
    pound, cut in half
3–5 teaspoons cracked black peppercorns
1 tablespoon butter
2 tablespoons Cognac
2 tablespoons beef stock
2 tablespoons strong brewed coffee
¼ cup heavy cream
Salt

Place the steaks on a plate and press the cracked peppercorns into the flesh on both sides; most of them should adhere to the meat if you press hard.

Melt the butter in a skillet over a medium-high flame and sauté the steaks until they are brown on both sides and done to your taste in the center (it is usually cooked very rare, 2 to 3 minutes per side).

Pour off any remaining fat and butter from the skillet and add the cognac. Turn the flame off, and carefully ignite the cognac with a match. The flames will die down quickly.

Transfer the steaks to a plate and keep them warm.

Add the stock, coffee, and cream to the skillet and bring the liquids to a boil for 1 to 2 minutes, or until the sauce it slightly thickened. Season with salt to taste and pour the sauce over the steaks. Serve immediately.

Serves 2

SWORDFISH STEAKS WITH GINGER, ORANGE, AND COFFEE

This sprightly recipe is a year-round favorite as it is light enough for the summer and complex enough for the winter. For simple entertaining, serve it with good chewy bread, salad, and a rich dessert like Toffee Espresso Cream Cake (see page 134).

 2 tablespoons strong brewed coffee
 1 teaspoon soy sauce
Grated zest of 1 small orange
Juice of ½ orange
 1 garlic clove, minced
 1 tablespoon grated fresh ginger
 2 tablespoons olive oil
Dash of Tabasco sauce
¼ cup + 2 tablespoons chopped fresh parsley
 4 thick swordfish steaks, about ½ pound each
Salt and pepper

In a shallow pan or bowl, mix together the coffee, soy sauce, orange zest, orange juice, garlic, ginger, olive oil, Tabasco sauce, and ¼ cup of the parsley.

Add the swordfish steaks and turn to coat them with the marinade. Cover the pan with plastic wrap and let the fish marinate for 1 to 4 hours in the refrigerator, or 45 minutes at room temperature.

Heat the boiler until it very hot.

Place the swordfish steaks in a broiler pan and broil them for about 4 minutes on each side (or more or less depending upon how thick the steaks are and how rare you like your fish to be).

Remove steaks to a serving platter and season them with salt and pepper to taste. Sprinkle on the remaining 2 tablespoons parsley and serve immediately.

Serves 4

VEGETABLES AND SIDE DISHES

COFFEE GUACAMOLE

I'll bet you're thinking that I went too far with this one. I know it sounds strange, but really, the acidity of the coffee does nice things to the richness of the avocado. Although you may not want to serve this every day, it does make a nice change from the traditional guacamole. Use the Haas or California avocados rather than the larger Florida variety; they have a more intense flavor and creamier texture. To choose a ripe avocado, look for one with black skin and flesh that will yield slightly to pressure when you gently squeeze it. Avocados will ripen if left in a warm place.

Serve the Coffee Guacamole with tortilla chips and homemade salsa. Margaritas are a nice, but not necessary, addition.

      2 **ripe avocados, peeled and pitted**
      3 **tablespoons minced onion**
      1 **garlic clove, minced**
    ¼ **cup chopped fresh cilantro leaves**
      2 **small ripe plum tomatoes, seeded and chopped**
  ½–1 **small jalapeño chile pepper, seeded and minced**
      1 **tablespoon strong brewed coffee**
      1 **tablespoon lime juice**
      1 **teaspoon flavorful olive oil**
Salt
Tortilla chips
Salsa

In a medium-sized bowl, coarsely mash the avocados so there are some large chunks and some smooth paste.

Add the onion, garlic, cilantro, tomatoes, chile, coffee, juice, and oil. Season with salt to taste, and mix carefully. While it is important to mix the ingredients well, it is just as important not to overmash the avocados.

Serve immediately with the tortilla chips and salsa.

Makes about 2 cups

ORANGE COFFEE BEETS

I adore beets in all forms, and so it was only natural for me to extend my coffee experimentation to include these bulbous beauties as well. Choose tiny beets that are uniform in size with fresh, bright stems and greens.

1½ **pounds small fresh beets, trimmed**
  2 **tablespoons olive oil**
  1 **tablespoon butter**
  1 **small yellow onion, chopped**
  2 **tablespoons brown sugar**
Grated zest of 1 orange
Grated zest of 1 lime
  1 **tablespoon red wine vinegar**
Juice of ½ orange
  ¼ **cup strong brewed coffee**
Salt and pepper
  ¼ **cup finely chopped fresh parsley**

Place the beets in a large saucepan and cover them with cold water. Bring the water to a boil over high heat and then reduce the heat and simmer for 30 minutes, or until the beets are tender.

Drain the beets and refresh them under cold water until they are cool enough to handle. Slip the skins off the beets and cut them into ¼-inch slices. Reserve.

In a large skillet over medium heat, melt 1 tablespoon of the olive oil with the butter. Add the onion and sauté until it is soft and golden brown, about 6 minutes.

Add the brown sugar, citrus zest, vinegar, orange juice, and coffee, and simmer the mixture for 30 seconds. Add the beets and sauté them, stirring often, for about 10 minutes, or until they absorb the liquids.

Season the beets with salt and pepper to taste, and garnish them with the parsley. Serve immediately.

Serves 4–6

CARROT RAISIN SALAD WITH CARDAMOM AND COFFEE

Carrot salad is a snap to make if you have a food processor with a grating disk. If you only have a hand-held grater, be careful when you make this salad; I seem to be unable to use a grater without grating some part of my hands to shreds!

I find that it is unnecessary to peel the carrots for this recipe. Just scrub them well under running water with a stiff vegetable brush. Crush the cardamom seeds with a mortar and pestle, or bruise them on a cutting board with the side of a large, heavy knife. The mint adds both color and flavor to the finished dish.

1 pound carrots, trimmed and scrubbed
⅓ cup golden raisins
2 tablespoons Coffee-Peanut Mayonnaise (page 249)
2 tablespoons olive oil
1 tablespoon lemon juice
½ teaspoon lightly crushed cardamom seeds
Salt and pepper
Chopped fresh mint leaves (optional)

In a food processor with a grating blade or with a hand-held grater, shred all the carrots. Transfer them to a large bowl, add the raisins, and reserve.

In a small bowl, whisk together the Coffee Mayonnaise, olive oil, lemon juice, and cardamom seeds. Spoon this mixture over the shredded carrots and mix well.

Taste the salad and season to taste with salt and pepper. This salad can be served immediately, but it is better if it is allowed to sit in the refrigerator overnight so the flavors have a chance to marry.

Garnish with the optional mint and serve at room temperature.

Makes about 3 cups

NUTTED WILD RICE WITH ESPRESSO

This dish has both urban sophistication and country homeyness. It is a chameleonlike side dish, completely adaptable to many different occasions. Although wild rice is expensive, it is well worth the money for its unique flavor and texture. And, just as an aside, wild rice is not actually rice at all. It is a marsh grass that grows in damp land along the Great Lakes. It is a distinctly American phenomenon.

I used pine nuts in this recipe, but feel free to substitute any other nut you prefer. Hazelnuts are especially nice.

2 cups chicken stock
1 cup strong brewed coffee
1 cup wild rice, rinsed
½ cup diced carrots
3 tablespoons butter
½ cup toasted pine nuts
¼ cup chopped scallions
Salt and pepper
¼ cup chopped fresh parsley

In a medium-sized saucepan, bring the chicken stock and coffee to a boil, and add the wild rice in a thin stream so as not to disrupt the boiling water. Stir the rice well, lower the heat, and simmer the mixture for a minute or two.

Cover the pot and let the rice simmer for 10 minutes. Then add the carrots and replace the cover. Simmer the rice for an additional 20 to 30 minutes, or until it is tender, but still al dente.

Drain the rice and return it to the saucepan. Stir in the butter, pine nuts, and scallions. Season with salt and pepper to taste, and mix well. If the rice seems soupy, briefly heat it over a high flame to evaporate some of the excess liquid.

Stir in the parsley and serve the rice hot, warm, or at room temperature.

Serves 4–6

COLD BROCCOLI SALAD WITH CUMIN

This salad is terrific to have around the house. It is easy to prepare, remains crisp and flavorful for over five days, and can be made in the dead of winter when other green salad ingredients are limited in availability and poor in quality. It is perfect for a party, as it can sit out on a buffet table for hours with no loss of appeal. And it is adaptable; simply alter the spices to suit your tastes and you will create something wonderful, I'm sure.

Make sure to marinate this salad for at least 2 hours before you plan to serve it. I like to make it the day before.

2 large or 3 small heads of broccoli
¼ cup + ⅓ cup olive oil
2 teaspoons whole cumin seeds

2 small garlic cloves, minced
1 teaspoon salt
2 tablespoons red wine vinegar
1 tablespoon strong brewed coffee
Pepper

Remove the broccoli stems and reserve them for another use. Cut the broccoli florets into bite-size pieces, place them in a bowl, and reserve.

In a skillet heat the ¼ cup olive oil until it is hot but not smoking. Add the cumin seeds and remove the pan from heat. The cumin seeds will sizzle and pop furiously; shake the pan frequently so they do not burn. Set aside and let the mixture cool for 10 minutes.

In a bowl combine the garlic, salt, vinegar, coffee, and pepper to taste. Whisk thoroughly until the mixture emulsifies.

Pour the cumin oil over the broccoli and toss to combine. Then pour in the vinaigrette and toss again until the broccoli is well coated. Cover the bowl and refrigerate the mixture for at least 2 hours, and up to five days. Serve it at room temperature.

Serves 6–8

SAUCES

It is unfortunate that the culinary world has all but ignored the use of coffee to intensify and complicate basic sauces. Especially with this year's mad rush to find new ingredients to play with—most noticably the Asian and African spices the are being infused into everything from custard to cassoulet—it is quite surprising that so few chefs have experimented with using coffee in a savory, rather than sweet, capacity. This is too bad, because the results have been quite exciting.

In sauces, coffee carries the flavor without the heaviness of oil and adds a smokiness and earthiness in a similar way to meat. A small amount can deepen the primary flavors of a dish while the coffee flavor stays in the background. If you think coffee might rejuvenate a favorite sauce in your own repertoire, just replace some of the liquid with the brew. Or consider sprinkling finely ground coffee into dishes as you would salt. I can promise that the results will really astound you. And just because I didn't think to braise pot roast or pheasant in a coffee mixture does not mean it shouldn't be done; it means that it will become your new signature dish instead of mine.

The sauces I offer in this chapter are quite versatile and generally simple to prepare. Although at first some of the combinations may seem very odd to you—as they did to me when I made them up—try them anyway. Coffee really does do wonderful things to savory sauces.

COFFEE-SPIKED PASTA SAUCE

This sauce is delicious without being intimidating to those who are not coffee enthusiasts. It will become a staple among your elegant-but-easy menus. The coffee takes the place of smoky bacon in this thick, spicy tomato sauce. Make sure to give a large second helping to the guest with an astute palate who guesses your secret ingredient.

In summer, when fresh herbs are cheap and abundant, basil makes a lovely substitute for the parsley. And a dash or two of Tabasco sauce will be heartily welcomed by the fire-eaters at the table.

Although this recipe does not provide very much fat per serving, if you prefer, you can cut down on the olive oil and substitute low-fat cream cheese for the cream.

This sauce is easily doubled or tripled for parties, and it can be halved for more intimate affairs.

  3 tablespoons olive oil
12 small, ripe plum tomatoes, chopped and seeded
2–3 garlic cloves, minced
  2 cups strong brewed coffee
  ½ cup heavy cream
  ½ cup chopped Italian parsley
Salt and pepper

Heat the olive oil in a large (preferably nonstick) pan until it is hot but not smoking. Add the plum tomatoes and sauté them over medium heat for 5 to 6 minutes, until the tomatoes begin to break down and release their juices. Stir vigorously with a wooden spoon to accelerate this process.

Add the garlic and sauté another minute, stirring constantly, until it turns opaque. Do not let the garlic turn brown. Add the coffee and gently boil the sauce until it thickens somewhat, about 7 to 12 minutes.

Pour in the heavy cream, and reduce the sauce until it is thick enough to coat the pasta. Add the parsley and season with salt and pepper to taste.

Make this sauce up to three days of time, and then carefully reheat it over a low flame or in the microwave.

Serves 4–6

COFFEE-CHIVE SAUCE

This all-purpose butter sauce tastes good on everything from pasta to chicken breasts to steamed vegetables. I especially like to use it on steamed new potatoes. For the amount of flavor this sauce produces, it seems almost too simple to be true. If you don't have fresh chives, use another fresh herb, like tarragon or thyme or even parsley. But don't bother with dried herbs because freshness is essential to maintain the liveliness in this lush sauce.

Again, feel free to double or halve the recipe.

4 tablespoons (½ stick) butter
1 garlic clove minced
½ cup strong brewed coffee
⅓ cup chopped fresh chives
Salt and pepper

Melt the butter in a small saucepan over medium-low heat until the foam begins to subside. Add the garlic and stir until it releases its scent and turns opaque, 1 or 2 minutes.

Pour in the coffee and turn up the flame to high. Stir constantly until the sauce thickens a bit, and then remove from heat.

Stir in the chives, and season with salt and pepper to taste.

Makes about ⅔ cup

Some other suggestions for using this versatile sauce:

1. Spoon some on sautéed veal and serve with lemon wedges.
2. Drizzle it on poached sea scallops.
3. Toss it with hot rice for an unusual side dish.
4. Brush it on broiled mushroom caps.
5. Use it instead of gravy with broiled or grilled steak.
6. Dip boiled ears of fresh corn into it.
7. Serve it with grilled tuna steak and garnish with grated orange zest.
8. Coat shrimp with it and broil until done.
9. Pour it on steamed cauliflower or broccoli.
10. Be creative; I haven't even scratched the surface yet.

ROASTED WALNUT PESTO

This pesto is unique in being both light and hearty at the same time. By substituting other nuts and herbs for the walnuts and basil, you can create end-

less variations. Make a big batch because it freezes perfectly, or can be refrigerated in a jar with a tight-fitting lid for up to three months.

Mixed with equal parts sour cream and mayonnaise, this sauce makes a super dip for crudités.

1 cup shelled walnuts
6 garlic cloves, coarsely chopped
4 cups fresh basil leaves
½ cup fresh Italian parsley leaves
⅓ cup olive oil
2 tablespoons balsamic vinegar
⅓ cup freshly brewed coffee
1 teaspoon salt
Freshly ground pepper

Heat the oven to 350°F.

Spread walnuts out in one layer on a baking sheet, and bake, stirring occasionally, for 15 to 20 minutes or until the walnuts are completely roasted on the inside; taste one to be sure. They will have a deep brown color and smell sweet and nutty. Cool for a few minutes on the baking tray, and reserve.

In a food processor or blender, combine the walnuts, garlic, basil, parsley, olive oil, and balsamic vinegar. Process until everything is finely chopped. Gradually add just enough of the coffee to make a smooth paste. Season with salt and pepper to taste.

Makes 1 quart

RED WINE SAUCE WITH COFFEE

This is a variation on a simple classic brown sauce and is amenable to substitutions and additions. The coffee takes the place of some of the beef broth for an earthy and unusual flavor. Although no one will be able to identify the coffee, your guests will notice and appreciate its subtle nuance.

 2 **tablespoons olive oil**
 4 **tablespoons (½ stick) butter at room temperature**
 3 **shallots, minced**
 1 **cup dry red wine**
 ¾ **cup beef broth or canned beef bouillon**
 ½ **cup strong brewed coffee**
 1 **bay leaf**
 3 **tablespoons all-purpose flour**
Salt and pepper

In a medium-sized saucepan over medium heat, melt the olive oil and 1 tablespoon of the butter, stirring until they are well combined. Add the shallots and sauté them for a few minutes until they are pale gold. Add the wine, the broth, the coffee, and the bay leaf, and bring the mixture to a boil. Allow it to simmer over high heat until it is reduced by half.

Make a beurre manie: knead the remaining 3 tablespoons butter and the flour together until they are smooth and well combined, and then form mixture into small balls. Drop a few of the balls into the sauce at a time, and stir constantly with a whisk until the sauce is thick enough to please you. Remove from heat, season with salt and pepper to taste, and fish out the bay leaf.

Strain the sauce through a fine sieve to remove any lumps and bits of shallot; this makes for a nice silky texture. If you plan to embellish it, strain the sauce back into the pan before adding what you will. Store the sauce in the refrigerator for up to three days, or use it at once.

Makes 1½ cups

Variations: If you prefer a spicier sauce for meat, add some Dijon mustard and a few drops of Tabasco sauce. Or add some grated orange or lemon rind moistened with a tablespoon of orange-flavored liqueur, like Grand Marnier or Cointreau, for a fresh sauce for poultry. If you happen to to cook some game, add a bit of sweet sherry or Madeira, and boil the sauce down to a glaze. Green peppercorns or capers stirred into the basic sauce at the last minute work well with hearty fish, such as swordfish and tuna. Fresh herbs are always a welcome addition.

"WILD" MUSHROOM SAUCE

Coffee makes ordinary white cultivated mushrooms taste like wild ones, and I highly recommend this sauce over pasta as well as meat. You may also add sliced or cubed raw chicken breasts to the sauce as it cooks, which will beautifully infuse the cooking meat with flavor.

2 tablespoons olive oil
1 small yellow onion, finely chopped

 1 **pound cultivated mushrooms, cleaned, trimmed,**
     and sliced
 2 **garlic cloves, minced**
 ¼ **cup white wine**
 ¼ **cup strong brewed coffee**
 2 **tablespoons chopped fresh rosemary**
Salt and pepper

Heat the olive oil in a large (preferably nonstick) pan over a medium flame until hot but not smoking. Add the onion and lower the heat just a bit. Sauté the onion until it starts to become limp and golden, about 4 minutes, and then add the mushrooms. Sauté the mushrooms for several minutes until they turn brown and lose half of their volume as they release water. Add the garlic and sauté another minute until the garlic turns opaque and releases its characteristic scent. Do not let the garlic brown.

Pour in the wine and coffee, and reduce the mixture by almost half, until it is thick enough for its intended purpose (thick for veal, thinner for pasta).

Add the rosemary, and season with salt and pepper to taste.

Makes 4–6 servings

THAI PEANUT SAUCE WITH COFFEE

Thai peanut sauce, sometimes served as a dip, is very often requested for catering jobs and probably ranks as my most popular concoction. The sauce is really very simple to prepare, once you have the basic ingredients on hand. I have made this sauce with all different styles of peanut butter and have found that my clients prefer a smooth rather than chunky sauce. And most of them were not as delighted with all-natural peanut butter in the sauce as they were with the regular. I buy low-sugar, low-salt, smooth peanut butter for the best results; however, use whichever peanut butter you normally buy, and this sauce will turn out to your liking.

Adding coffee to my basic recipe was certainly one of the best variations I have made on it. The coffee seems to intensify the nutty flavor of the sauce and draws all the flavors together. I doubt whether I'll ever go back to my original formula!

 1 **cup peanut butter**
⅓ **cup milk**
⅓ **cup strong brewed coffee**
 1 **large garlic clove, minced**
¼ **cup sesame oil**
 2 **tablespoons olive oil**
 2 **teaspoons soy sauce**
¼ **teaspoon hot chile oil**
 1 **tablespoon lemon juice**
 2 **tablespoons Chinese cooking wine (Shao Shing) or
         dry sherry**
¼ **cup chopped fresh basil**

In a medium-sized saucepan over low heat, melt the peanut butter with the milk and coffee. Add the garlic and cook the mixture for several minutes, until the garlic turns opaque and releases its characteristic scent.

Mix in all the other ingredients except the basil, and simmer the mixture, stirring constantly, for 2 to 3 minutes. Add the basil and allow the mixture to cool.

Spoon the sauce into a jar or container, and refrigerate it for several hours, or up to three days, to integrate the flavors. To serve, allow the sauce to come to room temperature or heat it gently, depending upon the recipe. Taste for the balance of seasoning. If it tastes too sharp, add a pinch of sugar; if it is too salty add more lemon juice. Once the flavors are right, serve it to your hungry guests and graciously accept every compliment offered.

Makes about 2 cups

COFFEE-PEANUT MAYONNAISE

The peanut flavor in this recipe comes from the coffee oil, which must be made with peanut oil. After mixing coffee into my favorite peanut sauce with terrific results, I must admit to going a little crazy with this theme. While many other endeavors never made it past the pan, Coffee-Peanut Mayonnaise was a superior exception. Spread it on smoked ham sandwiches with mustard and tomatoes, or spice up mild cheeses with a dab or two. Mix it with crumbled bacon, herbs, and capers for a dip, or make chicken-watercress salad with it. Use it anytime you would use regular mayonnaise in a dish that might benefit from a smoky, nutty undertone.

  1 small clove garlic, minced (optional)
  1 egg
  1 tablespoon Coffee-Flavored Vinegar (see page 253)
  1 teaspoon salt
  ½ teaspoon pepper
1½ cups Coffee Oil, made with peanut oil (see
      page 251)

In a food processor, process all the ingredients together except the oil, until smooth.

Very slowly while the machine is still running, add the oil in a thin, steady, stream through the feed tube until it is all incorporated. The mayonnaise should be fairly thick, but not as thick as the prepared kind. Taste and correct the seasonings if need be.

If your mayonnaise separates, you can reconstitute it easily. Pour off the liquid into a measuring cup and wash out and dry the food processor bowl and blade. Process an egg yolk for a few seconds, and slowly, with the motor running, pour the separated mixture slowly into the egg. The mayonnaise should whip right up.

Makes about 2 cups

Variations: If you have reason to be concerned about salmonella, you can still make coffee-flavored mayonnaise. It is even easier and quicker than the classical method, although you will miss the delicate peanut flavor and rich texture of homemade.

Simply add ½ teaspoon coffee extract to one cup prepared mayonnaise and stir to combine. You can vary the amount of extract to meet your cooking needs: less for a lighter dish of fish or delicate vegetables, more for meats and smoked foods. You can also stir in a little bit of minced garlic, which I add to most things at any opportunity.

COFFEE OIL

This is the base for Coffee-Flavored Vinaigrette and Coffee-Peanut Mayonnaise. But don't stop there; I have also brushed this oil on grilled summer zucchini with much success, and I guess it would work as well on other vegetables, especially eggplant and onions. I've tried it on shrimp, meat, pasta—you name it. It tastes great on almost everything, even drizzled on plain toasted sourdough bread. Coffee really adds another dimension to oil, and I wouldn't be surprised if some genius bottled it for marketing along with all the other flavored oils that are coming out on the market. However, until then, it is a snap to make, just requiring time, not attention. Use either peanut oil, or a mild olive oil for this recipe, as the coffee competes too much with a more intensely flavored one.

If you like coffee oil as much as I do, double the recipe; it keeps almost indefinitely.

1½ cups oil, peanut or olive
½ cup freshly ground coffee, medium-fine grind

Mix all of the ingredients together in a jar with a tight-fitting lid and shake well. Let sit at room temperature for at least two days; the longer it sits, the stronger it will be.

Strain well through a cheesecloth-lined sieve into a clean jar. Store in a cool, dark place.

Makes about 2 cups

COFFEE VINAIGRETTE

This tart vinaigrette can be used for dressing more than just lettuce. Try using it on sliced raw cucumbers, bell peppers, or tomatoes, or drizzle coffee vinaigrette on steamed vegetables such as string beans, red potatoes, zucchini, or cauliflower. Furthermore, this recipe can also be used as a superior marinade for beef, pork, lamb, chicken, or even fish.

½ cup Coffee Oil, made with olive oil (see page 251)
3 tablespoons lemon juice
½ teaspoon red wine vinegar
1 teaspoon salt
½ teaspoon freshly ground black pepper

Combine all of the ingredients in a mixing bowl. With a whisk or a fork, vigorously stir the mixture until all the ingredients are well combined.

Use immediately, or store vinaigrette in a jar with a tight-fitting lid in the refrigerator for up to one week.

Makes about ¾ cup

COFFEE-FLAVORED VINEGAR

When I first made this vinegar, I was ready to chalk it up as another failure because the flavor was harsh and bitter. I left the noxious liquid in a jar on my counter, where it got pushed back behind the mixer and forgotten about for at least five days. When I finally pulled it out of its hiding place, I was ready to pour it down the sink when I remembered that my father always aged his raspberry vinegar for months before he deemed it palatable. So I figured maybe a little aging had improved the flavor of coffee vinegar, too.

Well, it did. While five days was certainly not enough for a smooth and mellow mouth-feel, at least it no longer tasted like turpentine. And the longer I let it age, the more delicate it became. So, a word of advice: do not bother tasting your vinegar for at least five days, or you might not believe me when I say it will get better. Just let it age, preferably behind a mixer (it worked for me). The longer it sits, the better it will taste. I have one jar that is a month old and still counting, and it just keeps getting better.

I have also made this recipe with thyme-flavored vinegar. It is a nice change—slightly fresher tasting but not terribly different.

1¼ cups white wine vinegar
¼ cup freshly roasted ground coffee, medium-fine grind.

Combine all of the ingredients in a jar with a tight-fitting lid. Shake well and let sit for two days.

Strain the vinegar through a cheesecloth-lined sieve into a clean jar with a tight-fitting lid.

Allow vinegar to age for at least five days.

Makes 1 cup

SOURCES

American Spoon Foods, Inc.
P.O. Box 566
Petoskey, MI 49770
800-222-5886

Dean & Deluca
560 Broadway
New York, NY 10012
800-227-7714

La Cuisine
323 Cameron Street
Alexandria, VA 22314
800-521-1176

Maid of Scandinavia
32-44 Raleigh Avenue
Minneapolis, MN 55416
800-328-6722

Williams-Sonoma
Mail Order Department
P.O. Box 7456
San Francisco, CA 94120-7456
415-421-4242